Dr Sara Savage is a  y and
Religion Research (nd is
Senior Research Fell pplied
Psychology and Rel tions
to raise integrative complexity (IC) to address religious radical-
ization, conflict resolution, fundamentalism, young people's
spirituality, and the social psychology of church and religious
organizations. Formerly a dancer and choreographer, the influence of the arts is never far from her work. The developer
of IC Training and the Beta Course, she is also the author
of *Conflict in Relationships: Understand It, Overcome It* (Lion/
Hudson, 2010) and *The Human Face of Church* (SCM/Canterbury
Press, 2007) both co-authored with Eolene Boyd-Macmillan.

JOSEPH

Insights for the Spiritual Journey

Sara Savage

First published in Great Britain in 2011

Society for Promoting Christian Knowledge
36 Causton Street
London SW1P 4ST
www.spckpublishing.co.uk

British Library Cataloguing-in-Publication Data
A catalogue record for this book is available from the British Library

ISBN 978–0–281–06415–1

Typeset by Graphicraft Ltd, Hong Kong
First printed in Great Britain by CPI
Subsequently digitally reprinted in Great Britain

Produced on paper from sustainable forests

To Mark

Contents

Preface

In writing this book, I originally set out to impart psychological insights for the spiritual journey. Like Joseph in the book of Genesis, every human being will face problems in life: relationship breakdown, depression, stress, unforgiveness, bereavement and suffering. How these crises are negotiated, and what resources are grasped, shape the turning points of life. They are fuel for transformation.

Then Joseph's story took over.

Mesmerized by Joseph, I took two trips to Egypt to imbibe the ancient history and culture into which this semi-nomadic shepherd boy had been thrust so long ago. The oral tradition underlying the Joseph story in Genesis dates back over three-and-a-half thousand years, and is one of humanity's earliest and most insightful accounts of a human life. It was written down by priests and rabbis after the Babylonian Exile some time during the late sixth (or seventh) century BC. The story still pulses with visceral honesty. The personality of Joseph leaps off the page.

I believe Joseph's story sets out a life pattern for our own. Not that many of us will be thrown into a pit by jealous brothers, nor are we likely to become Grand Vizier of Egypt, but Joseph's psychological and spiritual journey foretells the struggles – and the potential for transformation – of our own hearts. His story reveals a new way of thinking and living – a budding mono-theism – that eventually grew to shape the Western world. This fragile shoot survived against the odds in an age dominated by powerful empires and their pantheons of gods. As I write this,

ix

the 2011 revolution in Egypt is at the centre of world events; Egypt shapes the world once again.

Using the New Revised Standard Version of the Bible, I have sought to faithfully follow Joseph's story in its entirety. Check out this bold claim for yourself by reading Genesis 37—50. That is the best possible introduction to this book.

In retelling Joseph's life from birth to death, I have taken some artistic licence in culling repetitions, smoothing language into the present tense, or simplifying the amount of detail. In the spaces between verses, through expanding minor characters, and particularly through empathizing with the internal state of Joseph, a work of imagination began to unfold, helped by some Egyptology and biblical exegesis. I hope you enjoy reading it as a good story.

At various points in each chapter, sections of psychological reflection serve to link Joseph's experience to our own. Developmental, cognitive, social, clinical, Jungian, counselling and pastoral psychologies are interspersed throughout, selected for their utility in bridging the Joseph narrative to our own struggles lived out in the twenty-first century. These provide additional lenses through which to view the unfolding story. Placing story next to social science makes a strange pairing, but I have done this to encourage the reader to approach the biblical story of Joseph (and indeed any narrative in Scripture) with many different layers of interpretation: imagination, history, personal experience, exegesis and a whole range of psychologies.

The Study Guide at the end of the book provides another layer of theological interpretation. It is written for both individual and group use, and delves more deeply into the transforming journey, interweaving Joseph's experience with that of our own lives and, in the third section, with the life of Jesus. The Study Guide also explores parallels with our postmodern, globalized context in which people of different cultures and world views are rubbing shoulders in sometimes uncomfortable ways. Wisdom is gleaned from Joseph's fruitful immersion in dual cultures, and his integration of contrasts. Finally, the book and Study Guide serve as a companion to *The Beta Course: A Pastoral Care Course for Churches* (see details below).

Acknowledgements

The Beta Course was co-written in 2004 by Sara Savage, Fraser Watts and Ruth Layzell. The course first explored the psychological themes that are now further developed in this companion book. Many thanks are due to Fraser Watts, the director of the Psychology and Religion Research Group, for supporting the time out needed to write this book, and for material developed from *The Beta Course*. I heartily thank Ruth Layzell, Director of the Institute for Pastoral Counselling, for her Beta Course contributions, found in places in the chapters on the birth of the social self, and loss and grieving. My colleague Liz Gulliford has provided wonderful material on forgiveness. Andy Swindells has provided real-life accounts to illustrate various points. Thanks go to my colleague Eolene Boyd-Macmillan for her insightful work on James Loder, and to my colleague Jose Liht for his work on integrative complexity. I am grateful to the ebullient study group at All Saints Church, Hartford, who participated in the development of the Study Guide and gave valuable feedback.

Sincere thanks to Philip Law, commissioning editor for SPCK, for grasping the vision of this book and making it happen. I hope I have done justice to all this fine input, as well as the psychological material woven throughout, referenced in each chapter's notes. It has been a joy to write this book. Any inaccuracies herein arise from my own limitations.

1

The Tent

The birth of the social self

The story begins – as we all do – within a seamless time. We hail from a warm world, without comings or goings, needs or desires. Our first home is muted, soft and fluid. Close and secure, yet without measure – vast as the starry sky. The dream time.

Abruptly, a strange force takes over our peaceful world. It presses down. Insistent. It comes, goes, and comes back again. Then it drifts away. All is well. The familiar, steady rhythm returns to calm our world.

Then the force returns, pressure mounting as if for battle. It balloons, threatens, becomes an earthquake.

The force shunts us around, constricts and crushes. We are pushed to where we did not intend to go, turned around and upside down. We cannot understand why. Our small hands curled up, our head down, turning our shoulder to the plough, but looking back, oh looking back.

We have no concept of time. It is for ever. We endure the endless, endless crushing. We fight and suffer. Severed from peace, without hope. The senseless pushing increases, destroys, and finally implodes.

At last, space and time burst in upon us, with the cold, clashing noise of an alien world. We are shocked. Expelled. Darkness is now the pain of light.

Our first act is a sharp intake of breath. We cry and protest.

And now begins our Herculean task: to organize the universe and become a self. How can this be managed, when our most fundamental experience is cataclysm itself? Will the cataclysm return? Will it?

If gentle hands soon hold us, the abyss lessens, and we focus on the safe sounds, the warm presence we dimly sensed before. In the dream time. The calm feelings are now linked to something entirely new – a shape. For a time we gaze without blinking at the warm shape, as the shape gazes back at us. And then we return to the dream of sleep.

Joseph's story begins like this, in the fragile safety of a nomad's tent, three-and-a-half thousand years ago . . .

This tent is already marked by drama. Joseph's mother, Rachel, is the favourite wife of the patriarch Jacob, a nomad, a Hebrew. Rachel is desperate to have a child. Her jealousy is inflamed by the insulting, incessant childbearing of her sister, Leah, who is Jacob's first wife. Rachel suffers the see-saw of being the favourite yet feeling profoundly unfavoured. She begs her sister, her rival: Give me your fertile-making mandrakes and I will give you a night with my husband.

Finally the unfairness of life for Rachel is overturned. Joseph is born.

In a nomadic life of continual scarcity, unfair is how life is. The Genesis chapters preceding Joseph's story tell of continual unfairness, continual rivalry over the scarce goods of life. Passionate Jacob had already worked for seven years to win Rachel as his wife. The morning after, he woke up to Leah, deceived by his uncle into marrying the older, less beautiful of the two sisters.

Jacob works another seven years to earn his beloved Rachel. He clings to her, his favoured second wife. And finally, Rachel's newborn Joseph gets pride of place. The ten older siblings borne by Leah and two maidservants now experience demotion.

In this distant era, a patriarch with multiple wives and con-
cubines shares his tent with the favourite wife and her children.
Custom dictates this. No one dares complain of their lesser
place, their peripheral tent. This is how it is. The women watch,
holding their veils over their faces, while Jacob whoops with
delight over his newborn son.

The swaddled infant lies on his rug. He is the centre of the
adults' care, of their comings and goings. Above him a shaft of
light dazzles. The blurry brightness sharpens around tinkling
objects swinging back and forth, back and forth. These tinkling
shapes are tethered to the familiar voice, the familiar hand, the
familiar smell. He has no words for these marvels. They are
magnificent – but they are not enough. His legs kick in unison.
He cries out; there is a rustling sound. Events happen to him
and around him in an unbroken stream. His arms reach out
to touch the firmness of the murmuring shadow above him.
He struggles for this shadow to come closer. The fragrance
now envelops. He wonders: Am I part of this warm shadow,
so that as I am lifted up, it really is *me* doing the lifting? Will
this flow of movement, sound and smell transform into the
familiar face – the beloved Face – that makes sense of me?

Joseph's world – as is every infant's – is without concepts to
organize the surprise of existence. It is immediate and visceral.
There is no system of thought to neatly distinguish what an
infant feels inside from what is 'real' in the world outside. Every
occurrence, every feeling, is unfiltered – equal in power to exalt
or to devastate. This is how reality is! We fully believe it. If we
are lucky, there emerges one unrivalled organizing centre, one
Face, the caring Face, that rhythmically appears again and again.
That sense of face is so vital it is Face with a capital F. What
joy when Rachel's Face appears.

But when the Face disappears, the infant's flickering sense of
being a self-held-by-another loses its mooring. The world loses

its mooring. What if there is no end to this dissolving, this anguish of emptiness?

The newborn is profoundly at the mercy of the dramas of everyday life. The Face appears and disappears. Rachel necessarily moves in and out of Joseph's kingly circle, as our own mothers did with ours. What a fall from our previous bliss. We resent this fall from grace and seek for its return. If we are woven back into relationship again and again, we are helped to tolerate separations. We develop a hope that separations are not for ever. But if that sensitive caretaking is violently, continually interrupted we can lose hope. Our connection to the Face is gone.

Joseph arrives unprepared for this world, as we all do. We emerge after nine months with very few well-formed instincts. Fresh from the womb, we have no chance of finding our own legs and going off in search of food. We are helpless. We are equipped mainly with a desire for the human face. Babies are primed to search for *any* human face, though in time they seek out the familiar special Face they recognize. The beloved Face is sought with more energy and vigour than anything else.

In that Face, Joseph comes to know himself – mirrored back with Rachel's smiles and coos. He comes to understand that he is a separate being, yet somehow linked to this smiling Face.

Watch a mother and baby greet each other as the baby is waking. When the relationship is good, the mother's face, and her sing-song words, say: 'Hello. There you are. It's wonderful to see you.' And the baby mirrors this delight back, as he learns, 'Yes, I am here. And I am very wonderful.' This Face is our building block. It builds upon, but does not erase, that first substratum – the separation of birth.

The American psychologist and theologian James Loder argues that the real threat of death that the infant experiences during the birth trauma and its shock of separation are assuaged only by the loving presence of the mother or carer – the Face that re-weaves the infant back into relationship.

This face-to-face communication between mother and baby gives us our glimmerings of the numinous, the holy, according to Danish psychologist Erik Erikson. Erikson believes that the daily morning 'greeting ceremony' between mother and baby leads to a recurring sense of a hallowed joyous presence for the growing infant. Our sense of self, and perhaps our first intuitions about God, take root in our early months.

We sense this yearning for the Face in the blessing that God taught Moses and his brother Aaron to pronounce when the infant nation Israel worshipped in the wilderness, having just escaped from Egypt and passed through the dangers of the Red Sea: 'May the Lord bless you and keep you. May he make his face to shine upon you, may he lift up the light of his countenance upon you, and give you his peace.'

Joseph is blessed. His mother's Face hovers above him; he knows her scent, her rustling sound, her firm hands. This Face roots him to the centre of things. He is anchored, and contained in his own body by the sure way the adults hold him. Thus secured, soon he kicks and crawls, tugs and tumbles in the safety of the tent. His chubby hands and knees speed energetically towards every interesting danger. The faster he crawls, the faster eager hands snatch him from the burn of open fire, sharpness of rams' horns, the glare of sun. When he laughs, the adults laugh. When he cries, the adults hurry. He soon learns how to make them hurry.

The richly coloured, rough-textured rugs of his tent are pungent with incense, his mother's thick robes tinkling with tiny bells. All these provide Joseph with an ample playground and hiding places. Soon he learns to call out her name. Then he learns his father's name – his *abba*, his own name, the names of his ten brothers, the other mothers, the servants, the animals. This is his world. He is the centre of it. It makes sense.

When his father Jacob enters the tent, his booming voice fills the space and commands it. A new centre now exists in the tent: tall, rough-textured, full of energy and strong scent. The woven rugs are for him to sit upon, the pottery urn for him to drink from. Joseph cries out to be melded with this new centre. He crawls with fierce urgency; he hurls himself at Jacob's rock-like knees, propped up against a cushion. He pulls at the long beard and his *abba* laughs and flings Joseph upside down over his shoulder as he marches around the tent, singing his songs. Joseph loves this upside-down world, and the way he can turn his father's kingdom on its head – by virtue of being Joseph.

Rachel quietly counters the uproar of tent through the power vested in her to hand out freshly baked flat breads. The rhythm of life continues.

If, as infants, we have been as lucky as Joseph, and have found our hallowed Face in our first carers, we begin to learn that we need relationships to survive. We become a being-in-relationship. As the new parent watches and waits for her baby's smile, she instinctively mirrors back that smile and, in the process, makes the baby's own experience more 'real'. When the parent experiences how the baby really feels, rather than dictating how the child 'should' feel – disqualifying the child's own experience – the child's own being solidifies. This tuning in, and reflecting back, which most parents instinctively do for their infants, gives the young child the gift of owning his own feelings. Without this tuning in and reflecting back, children tend to disown their own emotions. If others don't value the child's emotions, the child follows suit.

And so, as vital as physical care is for survival, even more crucial are the relationships that tell us we exist, that we are wanted and loved. Without someone to answer our cries, our distress mounts exponentially. Will that first cataclysm return? Will abandonment be final? It is not simply the infant who is put right when held in a warm embrace, the world also becomes a more benevolent place. Without relationship, babies die, medically speaking, of a failure to thrive.

Infancy is an experience poised between life and death. The prophet Ezekiel, preaching at the time of the fall of Jerusalem in 586 BC, grasps this. Ezekiel pictures Jerusalem, which symbolized the whole nation of Israel, as an unwanted, filthy, abandoned baby, rescued by God:

> On the day you were born your navel cord was not cut, nor were you washed with water to cleanse you, nor rubbed with salt, nor wrapped in cloths. No eye pitied you, to do any of these things for you out of compassion for you; but you were thrown out in the open field, for you were abhorred on the day you were born.
>
> I passed by you, and saw you flailing about in your blood. As you lay in your blood, I said to you, 'Live!' . . . You grew up and became tall.   Ezekiel 16.4–7a

Infancy is a drama swinging between elation and despair. Experiences of frustration, being ignored, negated or threatened can easily evoke that wordless, cataclysmic experience of being born, expelled. Life's 'No', via parents or circumstances, can open the abyss. The sense of negation feels overwhelming to the young child. The inevitable frustrations of daily life – the servant slapping Joseph's hand away from the plates of food – tell him that he is not the centre of the universe, that he is not omnipotent, that he cannot magically command the adults' every move.

Through these small negations, a young child like Joseph becomes 'boundaried', with a conscious 'I' to direct his own actions. It feels like another fall from grace, but it is a necessary one. And, as most parents know, 'No!' is chief among the child's first utterances in reply. With this sense of being a separate self, the toddler exercises his new but small powers and pits his will against those of his carers. Where exactly the young child deposits his precious personal cargo, his poo, becomes a highly charged drama concerning whose will prevails.

Conflict is necessary. It confirms that the toddler is himself, unique and separate, while his parents' 'No' helps him to understand the limits of his power, the limits of acceptable and safe behaviour. So, when a toddler screams in rage, he is ultimately relieved to discover that he cannot destroy the universe, or those he loves, with his anger. Rather he finds that there are firm boundaries containing him. What he needs most of all is to know that his anger does not isolate him, and that his relationships are still intact in spite of what parents and carers demand of him.

If the child's emotions are contained in this helpful way, the child senses he can 'be'. But if the child's rage or powerful feelings overwhelm the parent, then the child has to make a dreadful choice. He has to cut off part of himself – his deep feelings of fear, anger or sadness – or be cut off by those he needs most. If forced to choose, the child will sacrifice his own feelings; he needs his parents more. The small self is shaved by each sacrifice of real feeling.

A crisis point arrives. Joseph's sense of himself is profoundly threatened. Joseph is six years old, and the unnamed cataclysm returns. In the tent the adults anxiously hurry, but not towards him. Strange screamings erupt, then fade away. They erupt again, and again, intolerable sounds. Finally, all is silent. Joseph is rooted to the spot. The adults have no words to explain that Rachel has died giving birth to her second child, Benjamin, 'son of my sorrow'. To Joseph, the incomprehensible has occurred: she is no longer there.

Newborn Benjamin and Joseph are left motherless. The games and songs are no more. The rustling of Rachel's robes, her scent of spices, her sparkling black eyes mirroring his laughter are no more. The tent is now a strange tent, the world a strange world. He does not understand the wailing ceremonies for his mother. They do not make sense, because she is not there to structure them for him. He watches the ceremony with wide eyes, his face thinner, sculpted by shadows.

There is a new small stranger. Joseph recognizes something in his tiny brother's staring eyes. It is the emptiness he feels within himself. The boys grow up with this deep, silent bond. They hold fast to each other. For Benjamin, there is no other Face than Joseph's. Joseph soon understands that he must remain within Benjamin's sightline. This gives him a purpose, a task. But on the inside, Joseph feels a void, like the deep darkness of Jacob's well. Joseph avoids dark places now.

But his father Jacob's affections are not dimmed. Joseph is still the favourite son, and he and Benjamin still live in the favoured tent. His role in the wider family remains unchallenged. Over many new moons, Joseph watches as his favourite constellation wheels across the heavens, and he sees himself at its heart, the shining centre that gives it form and glory.

If the adults around young Joseph stifle his grief, his emotions are bound to go underground. They become so distant that they are hardly felt. Or repressed emotions may burst out uncontrolled. What begins in the happenstance of life for us all, in time becomes carved in the young brain's neuronal pathways. These predispose us to patterns of emotional reaction throughout our lives. If our strong emotions are felt to be dangerous because of how others respond to them, and if we are not comforted in our sadness, anger or fear, we may become insecure or avoidant in the way we attach to others. We feel we have to hide our emotions, cut ourselves off, in order to have a relationship. Thus our bonds with others feel complicated, problematic.

But if all goes well, as we imagine it did for Joseph in his very early childhood, emotions can be expressed without the world collapsing. Emotions can be safely contained. Strong feelings are not despised, nor punished. Then the young child can learn to express strong feelings. In time, the child can learn an important balancing act: how to express emotion *and* how to do this in a boundaried way that does not ride roughshod over others, explosive, out of control. With this balancing act achieved, the young child can join life, understanding the rules of relationship. Give and take. Fairness. He can have both his feelings *and* his relationship with his carers, who also have rights to feelings. Thus he becomes securely attached.

From this secure base, the growing child can learn to soothe himself. He can do for himself what others have done for him. He can learn to empathize with others. We glimpse this happening in Joseph's relationship with his young brother Benjamin. In happier days, Joseph's carers had safely contained his feelings for him, and now he can do the same, at least to some degree, for motherless Benjamin.

British psychologist John Bowlby believed that attachment styles – developed in early childhood towards our parents and carers – persist throughout life, affecting all future relationships. If a young child is securely attached to his parent at the age of three, he will be confident to explore his world, make friends and develop fully. Insecurely attached or avoidant children do not face life with these advantages. If a 'secure base' has been provided by sensitive, regular parenting, a three-year-old child, when observed in an assessment called the 'strange situation', is able to cease clinging to mother and to explore this new space and play with the toys, at a safe distance from mother. The child will protest with loud wails if mother leaves the room, but will run to her when she returns. Insecurely or ambivalently attached children also protest at the parent's departure, but when the parent returns, they are uncertain whether the relationship is still safe. The child may hug, then hit the parent, or cry and then withdraw. Children with an avoidant style of attachment have somehow learned that attempting to attach is futile. It makes no difference whether mother comes or goes. It will not make them safe. Nothing will make them safe. The child sits frozen, looking at the toys.

Fear was struck into the hearts of a generation of parents. Many feared that even a brief separation from their child would be permanently damaging. The picture since then has become more reassuring. Separations *are* painful for children, but it is the overall context of parent–child relationships that determines how separations are interpreted and coped with. 'Good enough' mothering that is basically caring and consistent over the long haul really is good enough. If a 'good enough' mother leaves the room, the child has enough trust that mother will return, and the reunion will be a joyful one. In fact, you can have too much of a good thing. Psychologist of religion Brendan Callaghan argues that 'too good mothering' that seeks to make the world seem 'too safe' can actually hamper a child's future ability to embark on the adventure of life and an adult relationship of trust with God.

At the opposite end of the parenting spectrum is the abusive parent–child relationship. If this is our experience, we may fear and avoid relationships as we grow up. Or we may tolerate abusive relationships because it seems normal: 'this is how relationships are'. We may even seek them out. This is the dark side to the power of attachment behaviour. A child will cling even to an abusive or neglecting parent. A dreadful cycle can ensue in which the child, when threatened, clings in order to feel safe, but the person to whom he clings is the one who makes him afraid. Better to have someone than to have no one. The strength of attachment behaviour gives us a way to understand how children and adults can cling to a person who does them harm.

When a child is frightened, he will rush to mother or father, as if for salvation. There is a long evolutionary history behind this. For animals in the wild, the only hope for the survival of offspring is through attachment, through clinging and keeping close to the mother. The baby seal that becomes separated from his mother has little chance of escaping predators. Predators know this, and seek to engineer that separation. Attachment is powerful in both directions between mother and offspring; both are on full alert if this attachment is threatened. A mother elephant, on the brink of dehydration herself, forfeits her own place in the herd. She stays behind, risking her chance of reaching the watering grounds, and repeatedly seeks to rouse her dying baby.

So important are attachment relationships to a sense of safety that where there is a conflict between escaping real danger and making contact with those who make us feel safe, it is the act of making contact that often wins out. When the planes struck the Twin Towers on September 11, 2001, many people trapped in the burning buildings telephoned their loved ones, even before trying to get out of the danger themselves. Thirty-one-year-old Melissa Harrington Hughes was in one of the World Trade Center buildings when the first plane hit. The smoke and the heat billowed, and she struggled to know what to do. She phoned her father, Bob Harrington. As the flames grew, she called her husband of a few weeks, Sean. Facing death, Melissa's impulse was to reach out to those closest to her, to express and receive love.

Relationships are what make sense of life. They provide an organizing centre to life, even in the face of danger. Without people who are close, children find it hard to learn. Why make the effort? A child has to have some kind of rapport with someone in order to copy them or listen to them. It is because of such relationships that we develop a sense of morality, as we experience regular patterns of cause and effect through our interactions with people who matter. A child repeatedly placed in foster care, whisked from one failed fostering attempt to another, experiences catastrophic upheaval, like surviving one plane crash after another. No wonder such children often lack the ability to control impulses, to understand cause and effect, and to learn from mistakes. Through no original fault of their own, their moral reasoning often remains stunted or disorganized.

Relationships, then, are fundamental to being human. It is in the context of relationship that we come into being, grow and learn. And what we experience in our early relationships is the raw material for our 'internalized working model of relationship'. In other words, what we've had is what we expect. We carry these expectations, and the brain patterns carved early in life, into later relationships, and behave accordingly. If we have been fortunate enough to experience that others treat us kindly, we more easily expect that other people will be helpful to us. These expectations are magnetic. We tend to attract the fulfilment of our expectations of others.

Relationships are potent, then, for good or for ill. We have been formed – and malformed – in relationships. For our relationships to become healing, people need to feel there is some mutuality in them. It is no good simply being an 'object' to another's outpourings. We need to be an authentic person of equal worth to another.

Traditional cultures, through the practice of favouring the eldest over the younger siblings, or boys over girls, place relationships on an uneven playing field. Today, in conditions of scarcity in the developing world, it is still normal for the eldest son to eat the best food, get the best education, receive the only healthcare the family can afford. There simply isn't enough of the good things of life to go round, and the family invests in this one child, at the expense of the others.

When Joseph was born to Rachel, the expectation that Jacob's eldest son Reuben would be the 'first' among his brothers was overturned. Jacob's favouring of young Joseph turned the normal hierarchy on its head, and all ten brothers shared the slight. Joseph, the demanding, attention-grabbing baby, fails to charm the older brothers.

As he grew older, whenever Joseph stepped outside the security of his father's tent, he stepped into the brothers' territory.

Any wrong move opened up a rich vein for teasing and humiliation. Stupid – don't drop that! Teasing Joseph easily tipped over to bullying; it was so easy and fun to do – hilarious really. It was the only way for the brothers to equalize the score.

The young adolescent Joseph, accustomed to being secure, accustomed to having his feelings matter, dreamed of being able to defeat this horde of tormenting brothers. Even more, he longed for their acceptance and respect. These ten brothers had all that he yearned for. They had height, strength, beards, booming voices, skills in shepherding, planting and tracking. More than that, each one still had his own *mother*. They had their beloved Face. Did not Joseph, motherless, deserve their special care? Did he not deserve to be loved? These were his expectations of relationship. His brothers' disdain rocked his sense of security. He hid his anguish. Bragging helped.

Perhaps Jacob is aware of the tensions between the older brothers and Joseph. He decides to act. He presents the young teenage Joseph with a woven coat of many colours. In a world of desert ochre, this is an extravagant sign of favour. The gift-giving is watched silently by the tribe. No one can now doubt who is the favourite. The acid taste of hatred is in the brothers' mouths.

One night Joseph dreams two dreams. These dreams promise greatness, fitting for a teenager with a blossoming but wobbly sense of worth. He exults in telling his dreams to his whole family. In his first dream, Joseph tells that he and his brothers were binding sheaves in the field. Joseph's sheaf arises and stands upright, while all the brothers' sheaves gather around his and bow down. The brothers' eyes narrow as they visualize this bold symbol – Joseph's imagined masculine potency. Ha! So he thinks he is the supreme male as well as being the pet favourite.

Joseph regales them with his second dream. In it, the sun and the moon, and the eleven stars bow down to him. In code, Joseph is alleging that he will supplant all the brothers by becoming the

14

sole inheritor of Jacob's wealth. Even his elderly father protests at this teenage audacity: Are we to come and bow to the ground before you, I and your mother and your brothers?

As if his dreams come straight from El Shaddai, God the powerful one! The brothers' silent bitter taste brews more strongly: Let's take this dreamer down.

Some time later Jacob has instructed the older brothers to take the animals on a long trek for pasture. The ten brothers have not returned for many days. Jacob is alarmed. He paces inside the tent. Finally, he sends out young Joseph to Shechem to find them: See if it is well with your brothers and their flocks. Bring back word to me.

Joseph sets out from the valley Hebron on his grand trek over the hill country, alone, excited to prove his worth. A man finds young Joseph wandering the fields, and tells him he had overheard the brothers say: Let us go to Dothan.

Near Dothan, the ten older brothers are toiling under the heat of the sun, searching out new pasture for the flocks. Joseph appears in the distance. His magnificent coat shimmers – a colourful liquid mirage, floating above the dry horizon. Floating above it all, just like Joseph. Even at this distance they can make out the familiar stalk of his too-long adolescent neck, his wrists dangling beyond the long sleeves. Growing tall, sucking up too many of the desert's thin nutrients. They are reminded: Joseph's coat has long sleeves; theirs do not. His is rich with colour; theirs are dull and rough-spun. The brute fact of Joseph's favoured status, his absurd notions of supremacy, are plain for all to see. The privately felt insult is a shared fact, and father's authority is now far away. The opportunity to overturn the unfairness of life has come.

The brothers look at each other. Under the all-slaying sword of heat, they are united as one. Let's get rid of the dreamer. Kill the braggart!

2

The Pit

Entering and exiting depression

Joseph's brothers grab him by his coat.

He tries to explain, but his voice squeaks like a mouse. He had come to find them! To rescue them! He, the young teenager, had set out on this grand trek, alone in the wilderness. They laugh. They rip off his coat, shouting. Everyone is shouting. His own voice is shouting. It's a joke; they mean it as a joke. His head is hit, from behind. Who? The coat burns as it is ripped off his arms. He worries about the coat. Will it be torn? His eyes are crying. His mother does not hear his cries. She is far away, asleep in Sheol. His father is far away. More hitting that he does not feel. The pain is stored away, for later.

His brothers' ankles wrap around his to trip him. The horizon jerks to vertical. His head hits hard ground. Ropes are tied around his limbs. Heavy bodies force his bare skin into sharp stones, his face pressed to the dry earth. He is trapped. His eye fastens on a small labouring insect while his fate is argued by the tribal court, haggling above him. The dreamer? *Kill him. Kill him.* His heart and breath halt in agreement.

More arguing. Reuben, always arguing: Don't shed any blood. But the brothers already smell blood, the taste is firing their actions. They drag Joseph and throw him into a pit.

He remembers little of the pit except the bright sky. A dark speck circles silently above. Hawk? No. Buzzard.

The brothers brush off the dust. They sit down to eat their afternoon meal by the thorn bushes, where the goats are grazing. Joseph cries out. Pleading, painting the scene agreeably, the colours of a joke gone wrong. Beseeching, brotherly. Come *on*. His voice rises, begging. *Please*, come *on*. More cajoling.

Now bartering – you can *have* the coat. Nothing. Now ordering – wait till I tell *Father*. He waits again. No answer.

He cycles through his armoury of persuasion once again. Why don't they answer? Sweat stings his eyes. His trussed arms hurt so much they are not his any more. He pounds his forehead against the hard dirt cavity. His ankles are tied too tight. His voice is screeching now. The buzzards can hear it. More are circling now. They like the high-pitched sound.

Why does no one answer? Where is the rustling of the heavy fabric, pungent with spices and myrrh, the warm fervent hands, and the feet that run to his infant cry? Silence. Mother is in silence. Slowly the sun passes overhead. In shadow, the pit grows cold.

At first, Joseph's cries were painful for the brothers to ignore. Effort was required to block out the sound. As lunch is eaten and the white sun passes its prime, the shrill whimpering flattens to a drone. The brothers doze. Now and then an irritating sound breaks through. Joseph's cry pierces the heavy heat, and then grows small and futile, like the cry of a small desert animal. The brothers exchange quick glances. Quite funny, really. The dreamer.

Far away, a tinkling of bells – camels. Reuben the eldest, always so smart, saying: Don't shed any blood – we can sell him.

Fate is a problem solved. The brothers are in agreement; they are as one man – confident, ebullient. They wait for the caravan mirage to solidify and come nearer. Ishmaelites, carrying spices, headed for Egypt.

Joseph again hears the tribal court above him, this time bartering with the Ishmaelites. The price is agreed, men to men, the usual price for a slave: twenty shekels. The brothers plan to slay some desert animal and bring back Joseph's torn coat to their father Jacob. Soaked in its blood. Proof of Joseph's sad, sad death.

No one hears him. No one cares. Joseph swallows his cries like vomit.

He is hoisted up, and exchanged. There is laughter, and rough bonhomie as he is handed from one tribe to another. The deal complete, the brothers depart, and grow small in the distance. The familiar clanking of the goats' bells fades at the horizon.

Roped to the caravan, Joseph rolls in rhythm to the camels' gait. Days of trekking. The white sun blanches all memory of goatskin tent, woven carpets, coloured coat. Safety is gone. Enslaving Egypt lies ahead.

He dreams in broken fragments, stories of forefathers. His father Jacob, his grandfather Isaac, and Isaac's father Abraham, their stories . . . Abraham called out from Ur, to the wilderness, to follow the great God, El.

But now Joseph is being taken away from this sacred place. How has he fallen so far out of life?

To fall out of life – helpless – into a pit. That is depression. The pit of depression is often built first from without – the wounds and losses of life. The current cruel loss, however big or small, may replay an earlier, wordless loss. The return of the cataclysm, the loss of the Face that once made sense of life. You are helpless in its silent grip.

The affliction is swallowed. You are what you eat. You become distasteful to yourself. Then the prison is built from within. You become your own warden, imposing prison rules upon yourself. Clearly, you don't deserve any better. You agree with your dull fate. Expelled by those who are joyfully living.

The sudden severance of a relationship, redundancy, the failure of health, the gradual erosion of love – these lay open the trapdoor of depression, especially if these events evoke past problems. You may cope bravely in the immediate crisis. But six or twelve months later, you are running out of steam. You meekly enter the prison of depression.

So it was for Joseph. His brothers' violence replayed a devastation as total as his mother's death. Twice his world was shattered. And all life is built on that first unremembered shattering, the separation of birth.

Oddly, small but continual stresses can sometimes be even harder for people than catastrophic ones. Here, there is no place for heroics, only the draining away of energy. Subtle ostracism in the workplace may echo past bullying in school. The dead-end job feels unendurable, just like a lonely childhood. The unresolved irritations of a marriage stir up the conflicts of early home life. Hope for the future begins to wane in the face of repeating patterns. Whether sudden or incremental, past and present pain collide. The pain is internalized. You are alone in your distress. There are no words. You probably deserve this. Look at all the happy people with their perfect lives. But look at *you*.

A protective barrier grows around the shameful, negative sense of self. The prison walls of depression are finalized from within.

Joseph has more loss in store. The journey through the desert finally ends. He is sold as a house slave to an official of Pharaoh named Potiphar, an arrangement not unusual in the records of ancient Egypt. Joseph is brought to the official's house. The animal smell of tent is strangely absent from this house of polished stone. Duties await Joseph in this large, baffling space, whose walls are lined with confusing images. He stands stock still, masking his anxiety, his stomach shut down against the smell of strange food. The stone floor is cool against his blistered feet. He notices they are bare. Where are his sandals? Were they torn off him in the pit? Or taken from him by the caravan so he would not escape across the burning sands? Those memories are collapsed in his mind. For the first time he realizes he is a barefoot slave.

Joseph is observed carefully by those who work in the household. What does he have, this foreigner, this new house slave? They see that he has youth, and a good deal of Semitic beauty. Joseph catches the quick weaving of their glances, the web in which he must try to find safety. He has no choice other than to spend his resources – his youth, his energy and his intelligence – to serve the new master. He resolves to work hard. He imbibes the rules, watches who does what. He listens to the strange language. He points to an object and separates out the sounds the servants make in response. He repeats the sound to himself. He learns, knowing he is watched. He works hard, seizing ways of helping others. The household prospers, and after several new moons he is promoted to having charge over the affairs of the house.

Joseph is stunned the first time he sees his master's wife. She looks wrong. Her hair juts out stiffly, cut off bluntly at the base of her neck as if by a sword. He has seen women's hair before; he had seen his mother comb her cascade of waving hair in the tent so long ago. Not hair like this. And this woman's eyes – the thick black lines leap out sideways to her ears like the wings of a startled bird. The amulets on her arms show the same mad eyes. Apart from these amulets, her arms are bare. She must have forgotten her cloak. Is she deranged?

Potiphar's wife savours this Semite's stare, and notices her effect on him each time he enters her sphere. She stares him back, until he is forced to study his feet. She is delighted with his paralysed gaze and thinks: this is what I dress for.

Her stare is a torch pointing him out to all the household. In this tightly run house, she is too often at her leisure, and the game of stares now adds interest to her day. At first coy, in time she risks repeated, bolder advances: Come to bed with me. Shocked, Joseph refuses. He will not, he declares, commit this sin against God; he remembers well the rules of his father's tent. He hangs on to the stories that make sense of his life. Its rules are all he has. He holds on tight. He is embarrassed by her; he is again the awkward teenager. She must be deranged. He stares at the floor, not at her. Not at her alarming eyes.

This posturing is a ruse, she thinks. No one, especially a house slave, says no to *her*. He is fascinated by her, she knows it. She charges, and tries to coerce Joseph to bed. She grabs him by his cloak. He flees the house, the torn cloak left in her hands.

What to do with the cloak? What to do with it? She needs to cover her tracks. Fear of discovery. The burn of rejection. These transform themselves into a cool revenge. She calls her husband and servants: Look, this Hebrew has been brought in here to make sport of me. He came in here to sleep with me, but I screamed for help, and he left his cloak beside me and ran out of the house.

Potiphar's trust in Joseph is thrown back into his face. His misjudgement is clear to all in his household. He must act decisively. They, in turn, know well the supporting roles they must play. Not a word is spoken. Joseph, elbows trussed behind his back, has no defence. He is taken to the prison where those who displease Pharaoh are confined.

Joseph's back slides down the rough prison wall. His legs are unable to support him, hollowed out as they are like a dry well.

We are hearing a story told early in our human history. This oral tradition, first told over three-and-a-half thousand years ago, so full of spontaneous, gut-wrenching honesty, now changes gear. From this point onwards, the story's visceral quality yields to literary device: everything that happens in the story is now mirrored, or doubled. Twice Joseph is envied; twice his garment is ripped off him, leaving him naked and powerless. Twice he is thrown into a pit. The duplicitous acts of Potiphar's wife are mirrored in equal reverse by Joseph's refusals.

Two is the Hebrew number of witness; two witnesses shall confirm the truth. Joseph's two adolescent dreams have unleashed the disasters that have befallen him. Pairs of dreams, we shall see, in time release him. The artistry here is saying something important about how the Hebrews, indeed all ancient Middle Eastern peoples, understood the world. These devices of ancient storytellers, and of the scribes who wrote them down centuries later, are saying: The realm of heaven parallels the realm of mortals. What can be seen in this world surely has its counterpart in the unseen world. They are linked. History is unified by a wise and sovereign plan so that what happens in the earlier parts of the story are echoed in the later parts. The world has an inbuilt moral order. What goes up must come down; history repeats itself until that equalizing plan unfolds.

But at this point in the story, Joseph is left with injustice and shattering loss. There is no end in sight. His situation is helpless and hopeless. This is how the prison of depression feels, as it did to the Psalmist writing three thousand years ago:

> My heart is stricken and withered like grass; I am too
>   wasted to eat my bread.
> Because of my loud groaning my bones cling to my skin.
> I am like an owl of the wilderness, like a little owl of the
>   waste places.
> I lie awake; I am like a lonely bird on the housetop.
> All day long my enemies taunt me; those who deride me
>   use my name for a curse.

Psalm 102.4–8

Depression is a paralysing shackle for the body, mind, feelings and relationships. Depression is characterized by negative thoughts about oneself, the world and the future. Such thoughts cycle through the mind almost automatically. The world looks bleak, others are hostile, and one's own self is a lost cause. There may be feelings of leaden sadness, or simply no feelings at all – rather a complete loss of interest or pleasure in anything. Our bodies grow listless and tired; thoughts become muddled, concentration and memory poor. As it progresses, speech may slow down. There's not much to say anyway. Many find they cannot sleep, appetite disappears, sexual desire flattens out. It is hardly worth getting out of bed. Keep the curtains closed.

Depressed people often shun social interaction, withdrawing into themselves. Or, their presence makes such enormous demands on those around them that others shun them. Such a negative spiral, once started, is difficult to reverse.

The novelist Virginia Woolf, who captured our human subjective flow of consciousness in her writing, suffered from intense bouts of depression during her later life. She describes her feelings of failure, loss and emptiness:

> Since we came back, I'm screwed up into a ball; can't get into step; can't make things dance; feel awfully detached; see youth; feel old; no, that's not quite it: wonder how a year or so is to be endured. Think, yet people do live; can't imagine what goes on behind faces. All is surface hard; myself only an organ that takes blows, one after another; the horror of the hard raddled faces in the flower show yesterday: the inane pointlessness of all this existence: hatred of my own brainlessness and indecision; the old treadmill feeling, of going on and on and on for no reason: Lytton's death: Carrington's; a longing to speak to him; all that cut away, gone . . . women: shall I write another novel: contempt for my lack of intellectual power: reading Wells without understanding . . . society: buying clothes; Rodmell spoilt; all England spoilt; terror at night of things generally wrong in the universe; buying clothes; how I hate Bond Street and spending money on clothes; worst of all is this dejected barrenness. And my eyes hurt: and my hand trembles.

True, more women than men suffer from depression, yet women are often more willing to get help, and to carry on with their lives. Apart from that, depression can affect anyone, rich or poor. Depression is usually associated with getting older, but in recent years there has been a marked increase in childhood and adolescent depression. As the pace and promises of contemporary life increase, so do the demands, and the unfulfilled expectations. Depression is a great modern affliction, pervasive and disabling. It is on the increase; we are ten times more likely to suffer depression than our grandparents were. Despite its prevalence, it is still quite common for people to think depression is a moral failure – chin up, try harder, be more cheerful. More floggings. This kind of pressure only makes things worse.

What causes people to enter the pit of depression is as complex as its symptoms, and includes biological factors. Genetic inheritance can play a role – particularly in some types of depressive disorder. So can certain chemical imbalances, for example, in post-natal or manic depression. The more marked the physical symptoms are in a depression – such as loss of energy, libido, appetite, slowed speech – the more likely that medication for the depression may help to restore the balance of neurochemical transmitters in the brain. But even these powerful physical factors are rarely the sole cause. Usually it is a confluence of causes: current loss, previous loss, our interpretation of loss, and how much social support is on offer to us. Human beings are complex, and depression is complex too. It is good news that we play a part in building the prison of depression with our thoughts, our perceptions of life, our emotions and our behaviours. It is good news because it is through working with these that we find our way out.

The cognitive approach to treating depression deals with how we think, remember and perceive, and it is one of the most effective ways of treating depression. It is as effective as drug therapy in the short term, and even more effective in the long term because it tackles the profound way that depression biases our thinking, leading us to recall selectively the bad things that have happened to us. This in turn helps to prevent the recurrence of depressive episodes, whereas drug therapy works only while the drugs are taken.

How we think, perceive and remember may not be the *cause* of our depression, but a negative cognitive style will sustain depression. Depressed people tend to feel negative about themselves, the world and the future. Depression exaggerates our perception of the bad things. Ruminating and dwelling on bad things from the past can keep depression going on and on. Cognitive psychologist Aaron Beck identified a 'cognitive triad', a set of three fundamental assumptions that trap people in the prison of depression. These are thoughts concerning:

- *The self*: I am bad, worthless, unlovable.
- *The world*: Other people are selfish, angry and mean.
- *The future*: Things won't change; if they do, they will get worse.

These thoughts are rarely consciously articulated. They rumble on, colouring our perception, biasing what we remember. People who are depressed tend to blame themselves for everything that goes wrong in the universe. All kinds of cognitive errors sustain depression:

- All-or-nothing thinking: Unless I get 100 per cent in the exam, I'm a failure. Either I win people's complete admiration or I am a total reject. No shades of grey.
- Overgeneralizing: If it goes wrong once, it will go wrong every time. That one error in my performance tonight means I will never, ever succeed.
- Focus on the *one* negative or worrying detail: The parking ticket I got this morning will ruin the trip to the beach, and the whole vacation.
- Positive experiences do not count; successes are a 'fluke': I may have lucked out this time, next time I won't.

- Jump to conclusions; expect the worst: When he walked through the door, he didn't smile at me; the relationship is probably over.
- Catastrophes will happen: The one error in my report means I'll lose the account; in fact I'll probably lose my job.
- Take feelings as facts: I feel so incredibly anxious, so there must really be danger. I can trust no one; my feelings say so.
- 'Should' statements: Unrealistic standards of perfection must be attained in word and deed. I shouldn't feel upset or angry. I shouldn't feel depressed. My life should be perfect.
- Personalize everything: I am at fault for everything that goes wrong. I should have solved my friend's personal problem for her long ago.

In contrast, non-depressed people have the opposite bias. They tend to recall mainly the good things, and to repress the bad things. Non-depressed people view their successes as *due* to their ability, and their failures down to bad luck. Non-depressed people feel that other people view them as OK – even when this is undeserved. But depressed people think others view them negatively and, alas, this expectation is often fulfilled; depressed people are harder to be with.

The aim of cognitive therapy is to help people think in a more realistic way. Cognitive therapy does not invite us to put on rose-coloured spectacles, to deny the bleakness of life, or to overestimate how wonderful we really are. The rosy-glow mindset provides only a fragile defence against the dark side of life, and it is always likely to break down. Joseph's teenage dreams were, at least in part, aiming for a greatness that would assuage his anxiety in the face of his rejecting brothers. The strategy failed and bit him hard.

Cognitive therapy is about developing realistic thinking. It helps people to become aware of their negative biases and assumptions, and to query them. Is this really so? Am I really such a terrible failure? Have I never done *anything* right in my life? Are others always *completely* selfish? The aim is to capture these negative thoughts, wrestle with them, and replace them with realistic thoughts, such as: 'Well, I did OK on that test, I got 80 per cent right. That's not too bad.' We need to do this in conversation with someone who can help reflect back to us realistically. We need someone to be our mirror, to help us come to see ourselves more realistically. Yes, we do have some redeeming features. This helps us to enjoy life more, because we are not continually sitting on the edge of disaster.

Our perception is always selective. We can turn that selective filter to look for the good. Faith is the effort to hunt for the blessings that God can bring from adversity. It's not about denying the adversity, how bad it really is. Joseph was forced to learn that the favour of his parents, the early blessings he enjoyed, did not protect him from catastrophe. The cataclysms he suffered could not be denied. But faith enabled him to find a radically different way of looking at life – truthfully – but from a larger perspective that leaves room for God to act. That is the meaning of the literary parallelisms in the story of Joseph. The tellers of the story are encouraging us to wait for blessing to follow on the heels of profoundly negative, unjust events. If we can adopt a hope-filled mindset soon after a terrible event, this ability to wait for something good to emerge out of the horror is usually retained for years. The hunt for realism, the hunt for the positive amidst the negative needs to happen now. This is what cognitive therapy offers.

It seems that Joseph had a habit of seizing the moment in the hope that things might get better. The Genesis account does not reveal the inner struggles of Joseph in prison; we are left to wonder. We imagine him sitting in the dark, surrounded by muffled sounds, the scraping of prison doors, the mutterings of fellow prisoners speaking a strange, excluding language, ugly to his ears. Sometimes the guards shout incomprehensible and terrifying orders. He struggles to learn the strange tongue.

Weeks passed, months passed. Egyptian prisons were well run; the harshness was efficient. At times, tormented nights may have presented Joseph with the choice of madness. Some around him took these routes, bruising themselves with their chains, groaning and shouting. Only death resolved the night-time agonies. In the early morning the warden would drag out the body of a prisoner who died in the night. Slowly the days passed.

Joseph finally did find some blessing; the prison warden looked on him with favour. The warden perceives that Joseph can be trusted. What small interactions passed between them? Joseph must have grasped any opportunity – the passing of the bowl of water to another prisoner – to reveal himself as a human being who treated others with fairness. How many small interactions built up over months to produce this favourable judgement in the eyes of the warden?

The prison warden makes Joseph responsible for all that is done in the prison. Joseph has not lost his capacity to believe that his own actions can make a difference.

Joseph is aware of two prisoners in particular: the former royal cupbearer and baker. Both had angered Pharaoh. After they have been imprisoned for some time, Joseph comes to them while making his morning rounds. He notices their dejected state, and learns that both have had frightening dreams that night, but had no one to interpret them. Joseph replies: Do not interpretations belong to God? Tell me your dreams.

The cupbearer tells of his dream of a vine, with its three budding branches ripening into grapes. In the dream, the cupbearer squeezes the grapes into Pharaoh's golden cup. Joseph provides the interpretation: Within three days Pharaoh will lift up your head and restore you to your position. Joseph seizes this opportunity:

When all goes well for you, remember me and show me kindness. Mention me to Pharaoh and get me out of this prison.

The chief baker hears this glowing interpretation and hopes for one too. He tells his dream: On my head were three baskets of bread. In the top basket were all kinds of baked goods for Pharaoh, but the birds were eating them out of the basket on my head.

If Joseph were simply trying to optimize his own chances of making alliances, he would not have uttered what follows. Joseph answers: This is what it means . . . in three days Pharaoh will lift off your head and hang you on a tree. And the birds will eat away your flesh.

The third day is Pharaoh's birthday, a traditional day for the rulers to remind their servants of their benevolence – through clemency and gifts scattered here and there. Pharaoh restores the cupbearer, as Joseph foretold. But the baker is impaled.

The chief cupbearer is delighted with his restored position, his spared life. Like many non-depressed people, the cupbearer perceives his good fortune as his personal due, reflecting his own worth. He does not remember Joseph. Let those who are fortunate forget the unfortunate, lest the shine of success in palace life is tarnished.

Joseph is left to rot. Does this not finally confirm that others are selfish and cruel, and that life will only get worse? What were his musings? To keep himself sane, he may have exercised his memory, telling and retelling to himself the stories of Abraham, Isaac and his father Jacob. The deep structure of those stories taught him patience. His forefathers too had to wait and suffer and hope. At times his memory would provide him with a glimpse of beauty – a desert hawk in flight, a sky strewn with stars – a reminder of a world still out there. Now and then he may have dwelt on the loving Face of his childhood, the image of mother/father now blurring into one. Perhaps he would have to quash that memory, lest his own weeping break through too brutally. Then he would conjure a more ordinary scene of the fires the servants built to cook the spicy lentils.

Over time, Joseph's store of memories begins to grow thin. He could tell the stories to the rough walls only so many times. Hours, days, months. No change. All is stripped away from Joseph. Colours erode, sounds grow distant and flat. His stories begin to fade. His mind blanks. He sees no end. He smells his own flesh beginning to decay.

From his cell mat, he watches the slow progress of a beetle, rolling its ball of sand. In his father's dry hill country, the presence of insects can herald disaster. Locusts eating what little there is. Here, the Egyptians regard these beetles as sacred, as a form of the sun god, Ra. Why?

He watches the beetle. Grain by grain the ball of sand absorbs the sediment between two stones of his prison wall. Carrying it away, grain by grain. Day after day. Doing its work. Joseph watches. There is nothing else to see, nothing new to hear, nothing to know – *no-thing*.

Over an expanse of unmarked time, this *no-thing* is exposed. Joseph's ordinary perception of life is worn away. Grain by grain, his normal urging toward the centre stage of life is being eroded. As a child he delighted in being the favourite. He had craved his brothers' admiration and love. He wanted to be the hero of his family, the centre, the star, the saviour. How foolish it all seems. All this is being worn away, carried away by a changeless fate. Rather than glory, his body is putrefying, just as the food is rotten, the water fetid. There is nothing else. There is *no-thing*.

At this low point, something deeper seems to be uncovered, a quiet presence that is not like a presence that Joseph can describe in words. It is not like anyone or anything – it is a no-thing in this regard – yet it is powerful, and warm. He understands this presence through the framework of stories he still dimly possesses: the fact of El, the God of his fathers.

He had known the stories of this God in his youth, told around the cooking fires into the starlit nights. As a young child, these stories were to him simply about how things were, unquestioned. Then, as he grew older, he heard them with new ears. As Joseph sat near to the evening fire, night after night, the heat would sculpt his face. He could feel his features outlined, defining him as he listened to the stories. His father's stories showed him where he was, to whom he belonged. The stories were near to him, making him.

He would peer into the starry night sky. Then he imagined himself from a faraway point. How tiny we all are, he thought, how vast is the world's canopy, decked with silver coins like a bride. He remembers a star dislodging and racing across in an arc, burning up.

Joseph associates both these senses, the close burning upon his face, and the cool, far-away stars, with the great God, El. Such lofty thoughts he had then. Such greatness in store for him.

But he cannot muster these grand thoughts any more. They do not work in this bleak place. They conjure nothing. In prison, there is no circle of kin to sit within, no burning flames, no stars. There is no-thing. His thoughts are silenced. This sense of El is gone.

Joseph cannot muster his energy. He now rests – in the prison darkness – in a new way. He glimpses that behind the brute facts of his life – and within this *no-thing* of his present life – in the silence, something here is greater than himself. A presence. This presence wills that he, Joseph, exists. It is different from the way Joseph wills his own existence – fevered, demanding. This presence is different. It wills him to be as it wills *all* to be, in generosity, in calm. This glimmer sustains him.

Joseph leaves tiny crumbs for his beetle, his sacred friend. May they live in peace together. The years pass.

Joseph continues to hang on, though all reasonable hope is gone. In the terms of contemporary positive psychology, Joseph has *resilience*.

Resilience, in contemporary parlance, is seen when a person manages to function well under terrible circumstances. Resilient individuals show a track record of 'making it' – reaching the developmental tasks set by their cultures despite the huge forces pitted against them. Against the odds, they manage some life satisfaction. They manage to get a job, or settle down, or find a direction. They manage to avoid falling into criminal or addictive behaviours, even though the forces are stacked against them. It does not mean that the person doesn't suffer inwardly, or experience anguish given the terrible events they endure. But they do not give up.

For decades, psychologists have struggled to help people who seem to be destroyed by traumatic events – locked in repeated flashbacks – reliving the horror, pain or humiliation, again and again. Trauma endured by victims of crime, or people caught up in war, violence, earthquake or abuse can produce long-lasting, post-traumatic stress disorders. The terrible events get stuck in the deep, more primitive limbic memory that first processed the horror – in shock. The events are engraved there, wordless, timeless, ready to be relived.

But here is a surprise. More recently, psychologists have found that trauma can, for many people, also elicit a surprising amount of trauma-related growth. People can grow as a result of trauma. Not just get through the trauma, but change and become more fully human.

Joseph grows. We, the readers and hearers of his story, are led to understand that the presence of El, later in Exodus declaring his name as Yahweh, *I am that I am*, has very much to do with

Joseph's resilience. But Joseph's personal characteristics inter-twine with his ability to retain faith and hope under harrowing conditions. People need something to draw upon, such as the ability to think through problems. Resilience comes easier to those with an easy temperament, or who have talents or beauty valued by others. Of course these help! This line of research tells us what we already know. Joseph, it seems, milked all the advantages he possessed, and this is part of resilience. But there are other ways that resilience can be stoked. Resilience is fostered if you have been raised in a community with cohesion and enforce-able rules of behaviour. Joseph's firmness in refusing Potiphar's wife, and his ability to hold onto his father's stories, was in no small part due to the firmness of his childhood, kin-based community. Yet what helps most of all in surviving trauma is having had a close relationship with a competent, caring adult in childhood – whether or not that person is the parent.

Thus, what we need most of all is someone who has loved us. The possibility of love is retained viscerally, deep in the heart and gut, despite all present-day proof to the contrary. Equally, it helps to have experienced the pleasure of mastery – through achieving, learning, doing. Children who feel they can be effective persist in the face of failure. They achieve greater success in the long run, perhaps not so much due to raw talent as to sheer grit. If we have experienced the ability to *do* things, to enjoy our own effectiveness, we are not lost. With those two slim but powerful resources, love and mastery, resilience in the face of trauma becomes a possibility.

These resources describe Joseph. He had joyously secure attach-ments in early childhood with caring adults. Despite the death of his mother when he was aged six, the story demonstrates he retained confidence in the effectiveness of his own actions – not least, because he believed that there was a structure to life. What is seen is mirrored in the unseen.

From this we see that extraordinary resilience and recovery from trauma arise from normal, everyday processes. Resilience is not about the spectacular giftings of spectacular people. It is mainly about the everyday relationships of ordinary people with family members, friends or teachers. And where those relationships in childhood have been deficient, re-parenting can be offered through youth workers, social workers, wise friends, ministers, pastoral carers, counsellors or faith communities. These safe relationships can provide the opportunity to relearn trust in a caring adult, especially if this person is seeking to model the caring of God. In such a context we are encouraged to practise honesty and self-disclosure, and to build a realistic confidence in the self. We come to realize that *some* people can be trusted, that our self is not all bad, and that we can do some things well. The prison door starts to open.

Despite his resilience, Genesis never shows Joseph revealing to others that it was his own brothers who plotted to kill him, and who sold him into slavery. Joseph does not tell the real account of his life to the Egyptians around him. All ancient Middle Eastern cultures were collective cultures, as many are today. In such a culture the individual is defined by their kin group, their social group. A person's character, hence fate, was understood to spring from the blessings or cursings that flowed from forebears' lives. In a collective culture, if your family wants you *dead*, you are unworthy of life itself. Joseph internalizes this affliction. He risks no Egyptian knowing his true story.

The picture is complex. For Joseph there is both an isolating, shameful wound *and* inner resilience: belief in his own actions, and belief that he was loved. In Joseph, the two are rubbing together: resilience and isolating pain. The psychologist Carl Jung declares that there is no birth of consciousness without pain. Suffering can strengthen character, deepen soul life, and bring a person closer to God. This is what the isolating prison procures for Joseph. The favourite son, centre of his own world, emerges from prison as an adult who now orbits around a greater, spiritual centre.

There is a link here with Joseph's gift of interpreting dreams. Dreams in that era were a coveted spiritual experience. Dreams provided a glimpse into the twofold nature of reality, understood, in that era, as made up of two realms. The earthly, material realm was understood as the realm where ordinary time, space and 'everyday' consciousness held sway. Mirroring the earthly realm was the heavenly realm, timeless, eternal, the source of all things that exist: the Great Time outside of time. Dreams formed a link between these two realms, and between the different forms of consciousness appropriate to these realms. To have the gift of interpreting dreams was to have a link to the eternal realm outside of time. Even for us today, dream content does not follow the rules of ordinary life. Dreams have their own symbolic logic that speaks to those who have ears to hear, or eyes to see. To the Hebrews, some dreams were understood as a link to God himself; they were seen as one way in which God spoke directly to humans. Joseph would have remembered that Elohim spoke to his father Jacob through the dream of a ladder connecting heaven and earth, with angels ascending and descending upon it. Jacob named the place Bethel: the house of God.

A person, such as we are imagining Joseph now to be, would be described by Carl Jung as someone who through his losses has ceased orbiting around his own small personal ego. When we first met Joseph, we saw an eager child and budding teenager with more than the usual amount of inflated ego. Clinging to this fantasy of greatness, Joseph was certain of being favoured in every way, materially and spiritually. Life had other plans.

Through enduring repeated loss, Joseph had discovered within himself a deeper psychological reality, one that connected him to God. This was, in every sense of the word, his salvation. His ability to interpret dreams was not a stand-alone gift. It came from his connection to this deeper Self. This Self (capitalized in Jung's writings to show its special status) encompasses the personal unconscious as well as the vast collective unconscious – which Jung understood to be humanity's unconscious repository of racially shared memories. These collective memories give rise to basic myths and archetypes found across many cultures. Jung considers that it is *through* the deeper Self that we have access to the symbolic language of the divine. The deeper Self is the *conduit*.

As believers, we draw near to God in spirit and in truth – and this includes psychological truth about ourselves through relativizing the demands of our centre-stage ego. Through this painful, eroding process we connect with the deeper Self. In Jung's framework, Joseph now has access to the language of the unconscious and its archetypes – and this illumines his prowess with dreams.

In Egypt, dreams were seen as a vital link with the divine. Egyptians had a sophisticated level of learning in many spheres of science, mathematics, medicine and engineering, but they retained a deep respect for the mystery of dreams. When the available science and medicine were insufficient to deal with serious problems, Egyptian priests laboured hard to understand the significance of dreams. Providing accurate dream interpretations was one of their crucial roles. Their lives depended upon it.

When two more years had passed for Joseph in prison, Pharaoh had two dreams that greatly troubled him, and he was angered that his servants the priests could not interpret them. The cupbearer, who knew what was good for him, remembered Joseph.

Pharaoh had dreamed that he was standing by the Nile, and there came up out of the Nile seven sleek and fat cows, grazing in the reed grass. Then seven other cows, ugly and thin, came up out of the Nile after them, and stood by the other cows on the bank of the Nile. The thin cows ate up the seven sleek and fat cows. Then Pharaoh awoke. He fell asleep and dreamed a second time. He dreamed of seven ears of grain, plump and good, growing on a stalk. Then seven ears, thin and blighted by the east wind, sprouted after them. The thin ears swallowed up the seven plump and full ears.

Pharaoh called for all the magicians of Egypt and all its wise men. Pharaoh told them the dreams, but no one could interpret them. The wily cupbearer said to the king: I remember my faults today. Once Pharaoh was angry with his servants, and put me and the chief baker in custody in the house of the captain of the guard. We dreamed on the same night, he and I, each having a dream with its own meaning. A young Hebrew was there with us, a servant of the captain of the guard. When we told him, he interpreted our dreams to us, giving an interpretation to each according to his dream. As he interpreted to us, so it turned out. I was restored to my office, and the baker was hanged.

Joseph is fetched from prison. Hastily his filthy, wasted body is washed, shaved and clothed in a white linen skirt. He is led through the halls into the presence of Pharaoh. The stone palace is impossibly vast; its walls dance with figures lit by bronze-handled torches. The oiled limbs of servants ripple, and seem to merge with the walls' figures painted with gold, carmine and turquoise. These explosions of colour confront Joseph's starved senses. The palace is designed to overwhelm, bedazzle and subdue. Joseph has long been subdued, and so he passes calmly through this glory, and enters the presence of the king.

The mirroring and doubling in Joseph's story now reach their climax. Two dreams had provoked his downfall in adolescence. Two dreams interpreted for the cupbearer and baker had failed to release him. The wheels of history had to turn twice. Now two royal dreams provide Joseph with his chance for freedom. He puts his life on the line as he offers his dream interpretations to the all-powerful Pharaoh.

Joseph says to Pharaoh: The dreams are one and the same; God has revealed what he is about to do. The seven good cows are seven years, and the seven good ears are seven years. The seven lean and ugly cows that come up after them are seven years, as are the seven ears blighted by the east wind. They are seven years of famine. It is as I told Pharaoh; God has shown Pharaoh what he is about to do. There will come seven years of great plenty throughout all the land of Egypt. After them will arise seven years of famine, and all the plenty will be forgotten in the land of Egypt; the famine will consume the land . . . the doubling of Pharaoh's dreams means that the thing is fixed by God, and God will shortly bring it about. Now therefore let Pharaoh select a man who is discerning and wise, and set him over the land of Egypt. Let them gather all the food of the good years and lay up grain under the authority of Pharaoh for good in the cities, so that the land may not perish through famine.

Joseph is certain. His dream interpretations are in line with what he learned in prison – that the deep silent Presence wills that all life should exist. Joseph 'works' the opportunity. The larger Self provides him access to the real resources of life. God is at work.

The plan pleases Pharaoh. The doors of the prison open.

3

Into Egypt

Stress and coping

—————•◆•—————

The world bursts open. A shimmering green stretches across the horizon. Workers are standing in the green mirage, bending from the waist, pulling out – or are they putting in? – fistfuls of living shoots. The mirage has the *scent* of water.

This *is* water, shouts Joseph's heart, despite the unbelief of his desert eyes. Such vast torrents of water. Not in clay jars. Not in goatskin bags. Not in dirt wells handed down from father to son, hard dug, fought over, jealously guarded. Killed for.

This water is alive, running, spilling into the soil. Joseph tastes the sweet dampness of the air. Who owns this water? Does Pharaoh? Joseph considers the bending figures – are they worshippers? Are they owned by this water? The water is called the Nile, and this is the winter season of flooding of the fields, *ahket*.

He learns that these irrigated fields, flashing in the sunlight, are reflecting their thanks to the sun god Ra. Joseph bathes his eyes in the silvery blues and greens – patches of delta – like scattered mirrors, merging as one at the edge of vision. The land is alive. Tiny birds chitter in mass, their tumult arising from towering, bursting palms. Reeds whisper along the banks. Insects crawl across the water's stretched surface. Underneath the taut liquid skin the water flows darkly. Joseph drinks it in. He learns that Ma'at, the mysterious female deity, ensures the harmony of this creation, sending the Nile waters to flood at the appointed time each year. The god Osiris of the underworld, who dies in winter and returns in spring, is the life of the grain. And now Joseph commands it.

Pharaoh has taken him at his word: the doubling of the two royal dreams surely means that the events to come are fixed by God. Seven years of plenty will be followed by seven years of famine. Seven years – enough to dismantle the divine order, for Seth, god of chaos, to disrupt Ma'at. Without the delicate balance that is the harmony of Ma'at herself, the Nile will cease flooding at the proper time, and drought will destroy the fields. The surplus grain that provides Pharaoh with his power and leverage will vanish. Seven years of famine – enough to take down a dynasty. It has happened before. Thus does the chaos of Seth ever reassert itself: pharaonic lines ended, remembered only in the worn faces of archaic step-pyramids, windswept, robbed and desecrated. The king's name for ever erased from the victory obelisks by those wishing to forget past failures. Chaos unleashed, just as it was unleashed so long ago in the Time before Time, when destroying Seth was at war with Horus, lord of the sky. But falcon-faced Horus, with his whole eye the sun, and his wounded eye the moon, spread his wings across the sky and overcame chaos. Horus takes rule over the land of Egypt, then as now.

Pharaoh grips his staff – in his hands resides the imperative for survival – for Egypt, for Horus, whom the king embodies during his reign. Horus' kingdom, ever hanging by its thread of river, is surrounded by a vast eternal desert. Order must be maintained. It is his divine task. Only Pharaoh can *be* Horus, and through his own person, his own body, maintain the divine order, against the encroachment of Seth. Only through ritual offerings and true piety, and through Pharaoh's body preserved for the afterlife, can Ma'at be preserved. The prize of all his effort is the Nile bestowing its yearly overflow, refreshing the soil, filling the irrigation channels. This is Pharaoh's stark choice:

drought, rebellion and a violent end to his reign, or maintain irrigation and life for all Egypt. He stakes his reign on Joseph's interpretation of the two royal dreams.

Grasping the chance for reprieve, Joseph plants the seed for his own future glory. Let Pharaoh select a man who is discerning, and set him over the land of Egypt. Let him appoint overseers over the land, to take one-fifth of the produce of the land of Egypt during the seven plenteous years. Let them gather all the food of these good years that are coming, and lay up grain under the authority of Pharaoh for food in the cities, and let them keep it. That food shall be a reserve for the land against the seven years of famine that are to befall the land of Egypt, so that the land may not perish through the famine.

Joseph relives the moment. Pharaoh removes the signet ring from his own hand, and places it on Joseph's. He proclaims Joseph as vizier over all the land. Can we find anyone else like this – one in whom is the spirit of God? – demands Pharaoh of his officials, the priests and priestesses who have failed in the task of dream interpretation.

Lotus-shaped fans waft cool fragrance while bowing courtiers inwardly fume at this handover of power to a foreigner, a shepherd of animals, ritually unclean to Egyptian piety. Soon, they hope, this age of Hyksos incursions will be erased. Hyksos and other Semitic strangers from the north and east, riding their chariots into the sacred land of Egypt, snatching power, taking land, posing as kings – against them resentment simmers. All such foreigners are unclean to the ablution-loving Egyptians, who daily immerse themselves in the cleansing flow of the Nile, and scrub themselves with soap. Even in the underworld the gods can smell the difference – the stench of those not Egyptian. As Joseph, shepherd boy, is draped in gold chains and fine linen, regaled as representative of the king, second only to Pharaoh himself, courtiers are musing on animal dung and impious invaders.

As the ceremony proceeds, Pharaoh leans close. Joseph meets the emerald eyes of the Ureaus, the golden adder adorning Pharaoh's double crown uniting upper and lower Egypt. Joseph sees himself, face to face, in this jewelled symbol of the Nile. Like the river adder, he feels himself transform: he too has reappeared after a long drought. He too is reborn. The ceremonial sistrums rattle, announcing the sacred moment. The flutes, bells and harps erupt. Joseph feels himself shed his desiccated prison skin. He emerges new, glistening in gold and pearlescent bleached linen.

As second in command, Joseph rides out in his chariot, preceded by shouts: Bow the knee! Bow the knee! He rides out into the drenched land, perceiving the water's brightness with new, jewelled eyes. He teaches himself the names of the things he sees: Nile, delta, flood channels, grain storage, corvée labour.

Joseph is at his zenith. He is thirty years old. The first half of his life he lived in the safety of his mother's tent, as his father's favourite, a shepherd boy, a believer in El Shaddai. The second half he lived in darkness, hanging onto a fragile thread of life. He now emerges to face subtle, social dangers.

His first night in the palace he nearly steps upon a scorpion. It scuttles into the cracks of the stone floor. The locusts outside are droning their warning: Keep your eyes open. Eyes open. Learn the ways. May El help him, as he did in the pit.

He transforms his outer self, accurately donning the image of Egypt. The painted reliefs teach him: Wear your linen thus, stand in this way – one foot forward, braid your hair into this shape, paint your eyelids with kohl, slant the line this way. Wash and anoint yourself, filthy shepherd boy. O favoured one, perform your balancing act yet again.

Joseph, now in *shem*, the season of harvest, watches as the labourers toil, ankle-deep in mud. They work in rows, linen wrapped around their loins. Bent from the waist, brown backs glistening with sweat, harvesting grain, so much grain. They bring the surplus sheaves to Joseph, bowing low, sacks weighed by the *deben* to be brought for storage at the temple, to pay their tax and to store the surplus. Joseph recalls the dreams of his adolescent self – the ten sheaves bowing down to his proud upright sheaf. His heart leaps; the vision is exact. His brothers should see this – his vizier's crown a punch in their face. But his brothers will not see it. His triumph is unmirrored.

The toiling peasants see only the exterior: the stately vizier, the vertical shaft of him, crowned with a headdress narrowing to its highest point. His tall silhouette, framed by the sun, is the inverse shape of the pit into which he had been thrown.

Joseph sees himself through their eyes and knows that, above ground, he is imposing and powerful – that the *fact* of him is accomplished in this land. He also sees himself with his inward eye: the shape of the pit and the prison are the shape of his inward soul. He knows there are two Josephs: the above-ground and the below-ground. He will make sure that only one is visible.

As vizier, Joseph guards not only a kingdom, but a split – a split between his above-ground self and below-ground self. These he must keep separate. His inward, below-ground self is unclean to the people he lords over. They must never know that it was his own kin who sought to kill him; the shame of the pit is too great, the stain of their rejection impossible to remove.

Joseph observes the skill of the workers as they flush the irrigation channels with fresh alluvial waters. The complex working of the channel system is beyond his grasp. He compares this network of water to the well in Beersheba – his family's pride, dug by Isaac's own hands. He imagines the creak of the rope as it brings up a single bucket, slopping, half-full. He hears a crack of laughter and sees two Egyptians splashing about in the flowing river water. Yes, they would laugh if they could see his family's dirt well. They would laugh at him. And his family.

Joseph still smarts from the steward's glance last night; even today he senses mockery in the air. The steward had sailed into Joseph's quarters at sunset with a papyrus scroll. Head bowed, he handed it to Joseph with a flourish. The corner of the steward's mouth twitched. Joseph sensed the steward's implicit challenge: Can you even read this?

A moment later he caught the steward washing his hands at the ablution stand – shaking off the water with ritual precision. His audience, two hallway guards, stifled their mirth. They knew. Joseph stormed towards his own chamber, face burning. He threw himself onto his couch, and squashed his face in his hands. He vowed to learn the baffling picture-words, but who could he trust to teach him? He felt the pit grow around him, once again. They must not know about this. Not about his below-ground self.

He sits in stillness. He remembers the silence of the prison. And the Presence in the absence, the no-thing, pervading all, willing him to exist. His heart grows still. The churning questions inside his heart are clarified:

- Whose stories command the blessing of heaven? His father's stories? Or the Egyptians'?
- Whose stories are right? The answer to this will determine who is clean, and who is unclean, the question that makes Joseph's face burn.
- And the question that hurts like a sharp twisting knife: To whom does Joseph now belong? To his father's tribe? Or to the Egyptians?

The tribal court that haggles inside his head marshals the arguments, one by one. The Egyptians have a miraculous store of knowledge. Their scribes know of the gods, their mysterious forms as jackal or as falcon; their alternative form as man or as woman. The goddess Nut swallows the sun at night and gives birth to it each morning. Thoth, a moon deity, scribe of the gods, with ibis head, gives knowledge. The Egyptian scribes possess the secrets of the stars, of measurements, of building impossible structures more permanent than mountains, secrets stored in the House of Books.

They have an abundance of grain, and vibrant markets – women buying and selling, calling out, bartering, shouting. It is clear that they have the blessing of Ma'at, whose mist blends at dawn with the sun god, Ra. These women buy land, they can demand divorce, train as priestesses, petition the vizier for justice. Even the lowest peasant can petition the vizier. He compares these robust Egyptians who live so publicly to the women of his own tribe. Other than the mothers Rachel and Leah and their maidservants, he hardly knew women; they lived in different tents, they were covered from the sun, robes billowing in the wind. He thought of his father's women sitting around the fire, saying few words to the men, but laughing to each other behind their hands. He remembers their high-pitched singing.

Joseph considers the Egyptians around him. He has never seen so many people not his own kin. Nor so many naked limbs. His tribe wears long garments against the sun, heads covered. Here, oiled limbs are the colour of pale desert sand, copper, dark red clay, or pure ebony. The children run about, joyously naked, until their maturity. In the marketplace, bare limbs weave and gesticulate in clouds of chaos; at the temple, in disciplined lines, bowing with reverence as the god is brought forth on ritual procession.

Joseph's eyes are overwhelmed. He is also faintly repelled by the strangeness of these people, the royal marriages between brother and sister, the shiftings of the gods between their animal and human forms. Even their sacred stories shift and mutate.

As a boy, he had heard that the power of this river kingdom is unrivalled in all the world. Egypt. Now he sees the extent of it. The physicians here know the secrets of the human body, of healing and preserving the dead. They know about beauty and joy. The music of their celebrations as the god is paraded from the holy place, their pageants thrumming with life, the wives of Pharaoh dancing for the pleasure of the chief god, Amun (also called Ra or Amun-Ra), their finery, the perfection of their gold and turquoise collars, the games of children, the graceful maidens whose bold, inquiring eyes force Joseph to study his sandalled feet.

Their stories tell of righteous laws, of divine harmony between the creation's forces of male and female, of the fellowship of animals and humans, of Pharaoh's heart being weighed in judgement against Ma'at's feather of truth. Tales of the afterlife, the jackal-headed Anubis come to convey the dead, gently holding the deceased by the hand as they face their judgement. Stories even more vivid than life in this present world. The Egyptians' knowledge far, far outstrips that of his own kin.

Their assessment of him must be true. He is unclean, a nomad, a shepherd of animals. He must shed the old and fully become one of them. But to do so is to plunge the knife his brothers meant for him even more deeply into his heart. And to risk losing hold of his father's Elohim?

Joseph's inner court counters; there is a shadow. The Nile entices these people into a life of hardship, digging fields and irrigation channels, year in, year out, planting, harvesting. Waging war to protect the land. In winter when flooding prevents work in the fields, Pharaoh's tomb and temples command work that is immeasurably hard. Work that too early ends vigorous lives, cut down by disease or injury. Egyptians, he observed, do not live long in comparison to his tribe.

Yet, when they are engaged in these great works, their vigour is palpable; they are a shoal of shining fish moving as one, indefatigable in their glistening, sweated effort. Joyful even, to create these monuments, their own personal toehold on eternity, into which they will one day vanish in a blink. Each wears the *ud jat*, the eye of Horus; each one hopes in its efficacy against Seth of chaos. They know the risks. Just yesterday, overseeing work on a temple, Joseph watched lines of men pull a massive block of granite upwards along the built-up, mud brick and sand incline. Heaving, dragging, inch by inch, upwards towards the higher reaches of the temple wall. The ropes strained, the men's feet scrabbled for leverage. Their legs trembled against the impossible weight. Suddenly a young man's leg-bone audibly snapped. He cried out, fell and was dragged off the line.

The men carried on, mustering their strength. The physicians would do what they could for the bone, if they could carry him, in time, to the *Per Ankh*. There, in the House of Life, the moon – the once-damaged and then healed eye of Horus – watches over the wounded.

Why do they do such work so willingly? Joseph has heard that the people hope to share in the afterlife with their Pharaoh. Even the priests cannot suppress this new belief, encroaching, as it does, upon beliefs once reserved solely for Pharaoh. Joseph's tribal court counters: What choice do the people have? Joseph knows how those who displease Pharaoh are treated. To commit a crime against the rule of the kingdom is to commit a crime against the gods, against the harmony of Ma'at. To displease Pharaoh or the gods is one and the same. Punishment is severe. There is no life in Pharaoh's prisons, nor outside the Nile's narrow line of green. The desert's dry winds suck out the moisture of life. The dusty desert, on either side of the Nile, itself compels obedience to Pharaoh's rule. Joseph imagines the sound of the baker's head crunch as it was rammed onto its stake. And so for the heads of all those who displease Pharaoh, or incorrectly interpret royal dreams.

Joseph has fourteen years to survive before his dream interpretations are proved beyond doubt. The fear in his heart and stomach rises. He has already survived lethal traumas, he has resilience and faith, but the long-term stressors he faces erode him like the desert winds.

- What if his dream interpretations prove false?
- What if the Egyptians reject him as unclean?
- What if, by becoming Egyptian, he is cut off for ever from his father's stories – the stories that give him life?
- If he doesn't become Egyptian, how will he endure a life of isolation?

The stakes for Joseph are survival. Physical, social, spiritual. Survival is the lesson that our human history – from prehistoric times – teaches us so well. Our brain did not develop first for thinking. It developed first for survival. Only later in evolutionary history did we humans develop our large, sophisticated 'new brain' – the neocortex which surrounds the old brain, and is packed with folds of neuronal synapses. The neocortex, the thinking brain, enables language, complex social interaction, and rational and abstract thought.

In the distant past, our old brain – the brain stem and the middle part of the brain called the limbic system – developed through the fittest and fastest among us surviving and reproducing. We possess a powerful, automatic stress response today because of how the old brain's stress response enabled humans to survive when under threat. In a situation of danger – a sabre-toothed tiger attacking – the old brain sent out instant messages to the whole body: Prepare for action!

Muscles tense, the liver releases sugar into the bloodstream for a burst of energy to the muscles, the heart beats faster, blood pressure rises, pupils dilate to rapidly take in visual information. Blood-clotting increases in case of injury. The stomach is deprived of blood supply – now is not the time for digestion – dump any excess intestinal baggage now! Survival is at stake. Fight, flee or freeze and play dead.

Survival rules. These processes are with us today. The old brain has only primitive, simple categories at its disposal such as friend or foe, mate or offspring. Thus the old brain responds to any threat to our social sense of self in the same way as if to physical threat. Our old brain is ever on its guard for danger, but it is not able to use words. When our emotional brain screams 'danger', it cannot distinguish a charging sabre-toothed tiger from an angry boss. It simply shouts – loudly.

This rapid build-up of stress hormones in response to threat works well if our social context allows us to fight back or flee for our lives. Thus we burn off excess adrenaline, cortisol and blood sugar. But if our social context requires us like Joseph to manage the social dangers and to hide the fearful split between above-ground and below-ground self, the attrition mounts. We store up abnormal levels of stress hormones.

Each person reacts to stress differently. Some people have a less 'labile' central nervous system, according to experimental psychologist Hans Eysenck, and are naturally less bothered by threatening events. When the door slams, they do not jump out of their seats. Others of us have a central nervous system that is more sensitive to negative events. One person's stress may be another person's challenge. What is crucial is how we interpret and respond to stress.

As well, each person has learned, from the reactions of others around them, a different emotional style. Emotional under-reactors bottle it all up. The people around them have influenced them this way, and now they keep silent no matter what they feel, cut off from their own feelings. If this describes us, we may lock ourselves in a darkened room dosed up with painkillers. On the other hand, if we are over-reactors, we may send flaming emails, erupt into road rage, shout at our children, throw plates at the wall. We may take a combination of both these styles. Either way, our reaction to stress often makes things worse. We can't think straight. We make poor decisions, we misinterpret people, we make mistakes at work. We get fired.

Then we get ill. Unchecked, the stress response erodes, first our immune system, and then our bodily organs depending on which weaknesses we may have genetically inherited. We may be prone to a racing heart, migraine, asthma, or acid reflux. These symptoms of stress are showing up in the areas of our inherited weakness. Over time, they can become permanent features of life: angina, high blood pressure, chronic bronchitis, stomach ulcers. Somewhere between 80 and 90 per cent of all medical conditions are now acknowledged to be stress-related. Stress makes everything worse.

In all this, it helps to know that each one of us has a powerful but inarticulate old brain that is part of who we are. This old brain means well; it is programmed to enable us to survive if threatened. But, like a wild elephant, it can go on the rampage. Some part of us that we can't directly control is acting out. The old brain is convincing, fast and powerful, but it is not nuanced. It is inextricably part of us, but in some ways it has a life of its own.

A critical part of this emotional, limbic brain is the small, almond-shaped amygdala. The amygdala is the home of anxiety and fear. Fear is saying: Something is wrong! Research by neuroscientist Joseph E. LeDoux shows that the thinking brain's neuronal messages are weaker and slower than the messages of the amygdala. So, fear, and the anger that arises from fear, can easily overrule thinking; they really do shout louder. That is why it is so hard to will away these powerful emotions. When we are in their grip, we are perceiving the world through vision coloured by stress hormones, and through the limbic system's basic, primitive categories: enemy, rival. Our cognition becomes much simpler as a result. We are convinced this is how it really is. We act on our constricted perceptions, causing others to react to us in kind. Conflict spirals upward in a series of mutually threatening reactions. Hormones and other long-acting chemicals released into the body during fear or anger can return to the brain and lock it into that state. It's war.

St Paul says: I can will what is right but I cannot do it. The Bible is honest about the sense we have that not all parts of us are under our conscious control. We cannot simply will away our 'lower nature', as the New Testament terms it. If we are in the grip of our old brain's anger, fear or anxiety, it is very hard to get it under control. When Cain was lethally jealous of Abel, God spoke to him using the metaphor of a wild beast: Sin is crouching at your door; it wants to master you; you must master it.

As humans, we face a demanding task: getting the old brain harnessed. It's like an elephant – we need its power to respond to danger, but it can go on the rampage. To stand up to evil or wrong takes huge energy, so we need our 'elephant' in order to counter wrong. But we have to calm this elephant, and turn its power towards constructive, intelligent uses. This requires arduous self-discipline and self-understanding, undertaken well in *advance* of threatening events.

In this regard, Joseph may be better equipped than us moderns when it comes to dealing with stress. Religious disciplines from ancient times had this implicit goal: calming the elephant. Prayer and meditation are both effective ways of influencing brain states. This is evidenced in many studies of transformed brain states resulting from prayer and meditation (called 'alpha' states). The sense of calm and peace that people report are related to real, measurable changes in the brain. Prayer and meditation can actually enable us to turn the power of the old brain into positive change through quieting the elephant, and allowing more of the thinking brain to dominate. This enables effective problem-solving because we are able to perceive more of the reality of our situation. Our problem-solving is usually more effective when we can see reality in all its complexity.

How did Joseph cope with the many layers of stress in his life? All pre-modern cultures were religious. Ritual and prayer were part of daily life. Ritual wove people together as one, dissolving differences in the face of the afterlife, helping them to prepare for death's inevitability, protected from fear by a strong mesh of beliefs.

For us moderns, death is usually farther away. More often we use prayer as a workshop in which to face *life*, and to deal with stress. Prayer can help us discern when direct action is likely to fail, when it may be necessary to keep still and wait for God to act. In prayer, we face not only our real-life problems, but also our deep-down motives, feelings, desires. As we persist in prayer when no answer seems to come, we are forced to wrestle with our deeper selves.

- Why do I want this so badly?
- What will happen if I don't get it?
- What does God want of me in this situation?
- How might he help me in this problem?
- How do I need to change?

When we change inside, the chemistry of our interaction with the 'threatening other' also changes. Indirectly, we spark change in real-life situations by changing ourselves. But this will take time to play out. Persistent prayer means we take responsibility for ourselves, yet we are not alone. We are supported, as Joseph felt supported in the bleakness of prison, armed with a clearer sense of how things really are, and the Presence that underlies the flow of events.

The empirical evidence is quite clear. Religious practice, even today in our secular context, provides people with resources to deal with stress. Some of these resources come from the social and practical support given by a faith community, and the social protection from destructive addictions they often confer. But that is not all. Having an overarching framework of meaning, and enriching habits such as prayer, are linked to greater levels of well-being in the face of major stressors such as serious illness or bereavement.

Yet, not all religious coping styles are equally beneficial in all situations. The psychologist of religion Kenneth Pargament has identified different styles of religious coping. Some people take a passive role in coping with problems, leaving the resolution of the problem completely to God: If I get well from this cancer, well then, that is what God wills, even if I ignore medical advice. Other people take matters more into their own hands: This is my problem and I had better solve it on my own. A third style, called collaborative religious coping, is a combination of both extremes: I approach this problem collaboratively *with God*; together we will work on this. Research supports better long-term outcomes for the collaborative, more complex religious coping style that is neither totally fatalistic nor totally independent. Coping styles are undoubtedly related to the kind of religious teaching in which we are immersed, and this research suggests that we need to be free to critique what kind of religious coping we are being taught.

We need to make some sustained effort at calming the elephant – whether through religious coping on its own, or in combination with common-sense coping skills. Common-sense coping skills seek to assuage destructive stress reactions at all levels of our being – body, mind, emotions, relationships. They include:

- Changing to a healthy diet,
- Getting daily exercise,
- Joining a support group,
- Learning to express emotion,
- Receiving counselling,
- Learning to be 'mindful' in the present moment,
- Taking an assertiveness course,
- Getting a life coach, or
- Learning new work skills so that we can attain realistic goals.

These common-sense strategies, singly, or even better, synergistically, can help to reverse the stress cycle. They can be undertaken along with spiritual means of coping, which provide an overarching framework to make sense of our lives. Whether using religious or common-sense strategies, or both, we need to calm our 'elephant' so that we can think more accurately. Otherwise, fear and threat will produce cognitive constriction. Our thinking shrinks down. It becomes more primitive, less complex – and presents us with choices as if they are black and white. Our boss whom we earlier saw as 'basically a good guy but he's got a bit of a temper' is now perceived as 'a total bastard who is out to destroy me, an enemy'. We consider our own and others' social groups in the same way. My group is good; your group is bad. We have truth; you have lies. This kind of black-and-white thinking indicates that we are seeing the world through the primitive brain's basic, blunt categories: I am right, you are wrong. Anyone not with me is against me. We become absolutist concerning our position. This is how it is. We cannot see that any other viewpoint has any validity *whatsoever*.

At this point in the story, we imagine Joseph being vulnerable to cognitive constriction produced by the layers of stressors in his life. We imagine him feeling that his life is presenting him with two choices: Egypt or El. His choices seem black or white, with no shades of grey. Either the stories of the Egyptians are right, or his father's are right.

The haggling in Joseph's mind continues. His father's stories are so different from the mysterious myths of the Egyptians. Stories told and retold around the evening fire. His father's stories are about the lives of those who follow El Shaddai. Sometimes they are about such small events, like being hungry enough to sell your birthright for a bowl of stew. The needs of a nomadic pastoralist are not a mystery: the shepherd of animals needs land and many descendants. This is what the great El has promised Abraham. Three generations later, the kin group is still hoping in these promises, yet to be fulfilled. Joseph marshals the stories and tries to put them into their correct order. Abraham was called to come out of the city of Ur of the Chaldees, to journey to a land he would be shown. Ur, like Egypt, also has storehouses where knowledge is remembered, filled with tablets of clay. Ur also has buildings more massive than mountains. One huge complex is dedicated to the worship of the moon god Sin. Hush, these things must not be spoken of, commands his mother – from her resting place in Sheol.

Joseph continues to line up the stories. His forefather Abram was given a new name, Abraham – he will be a father of nations, because his trust in Elohim has proved absolute, even if commanded to slay his promised son. The people of Abraham keep on following, though two generations later they are no closer to owning any land in Canaan beyond Sarah's burial cave at Mamre.

The stories teach of marriage. Joseph considers how Abraham's son Isaac – the son of promise – was given a wife from among Abraham's own people. His father's servant had travelled to find Isaac a wife from among their relatives. Rebecca drew water for the camels – a sure sign that she would be Isaac's wife. When

Isaac saw Rebecca, he wept, saying: Surely you are my bone and my flesh. And he was comforted in the death of his mother Sarah.

Such small stories, speaking of fidelity. Stories that bring relief from the fear of aloneness through trust in the unseen God. Stories of real people with flaws and, at times, serious wrong-doing. Joseph's father Jacob was a deceiver – he had deceived his own elder brother Esau into handing over his birthright. Jacob stole the blessing of the firstborn. Jacob fled from his brother's murderous rage. Much later, Jacob wrestled with the Messenger who would not release him until Jacob determined to negotiate peace with Esau. Jacob limped henceforth.

Esau, the wild one, the hunter, married outside Abraham's tribe, taking women from among the Canaanites – believers in the god of storms, Baal, and the female deity, Ashtaroth. The lives of Isaac and Rebecca were made bitter by this.

It had been commanded: Do not take a wife from among the Canaanites, but from your own people. Over and over again the stories command: Return to the land of your ancestors, to a land that I will show you.

How will Joseph find a bride from among his own people, so far away? How will he ever return? Surely Joseph is cut off from his land and his kin. He is a dry tree. Aloneness is a social death, a death of one's *ba* (soul) and *ka* (soul's energy), as well as the death of one's family line. His father's people seem farther and farther away. There is no way back. He is alone in his distress.

At dawn the next day Joseph watches the lotus flowers open to the sun. The blossoms rise and fall, as the Nile water gently surges towards the sea. The blossoms are shaped like maidens' hands seen on wall carvings – palms cupped, raised to bless the gods. Joseph has studied many wall carvings by now; he has learned to read the pictures. He once saw a wall carving – a man and wife – the woman's hand upturned, the man's hand touching with infinite delicacy the centre of her palm. Joseph has no maiden.

He watches two pale butterflies tumbling, weaving their dance in mid-air, coming to rest on a lotus flower. He thinks of his young brother Benjamin, and the day of his birth when Joseph's world ended and Rachel was no more. But then, he remembers the games they played together in the tent. Rolling and tussling, laughing and shouting. A former life, long ago, with smells of animal skin, woollen dyes, and his brother's musty head nestled in the crook of his arm.

The butterflies part – they zigzag joyously. One comes to rest on Joseph's forearm, on his bare skin, the part not covered with vizier's gold. Antennae waving, Joseph imagines she is greeting him. He holds still, drinking in the lightest of touch. Other insects are landing on him – an emerald dragonfly, a locust, a honey wasp. The kindness of insects – to greet him in this way.

Suddenly Joseph is ravenous – for touch. No one has touched him since his rebirth as vizier. The servants avoid his touch. Courtiers swiftly sidestep when he passes, hinting: Unclean. Workers dare not come near. And of course, he must not touch the king; no one touches the king. To all Egyptians he is unclean. He feels his body fading away from his heart, becoming translucent like an adder's dead skin, leaving only his vizier's garment to inhabit the physical space in which he moves.

Pharaoh perceives this. It is a problem for his reign. He needs his people to obey Joseph, to treat him as clean. Pharaoh alone has the power to rewrite religious reality. He considers which god he can select for Joseph's merging: not Amun, too awesome, not Osiris, too beloved, not Horus, for he is royal. He selects the less-important sun-disk god, Anu. Pharaoh can imagine this deity being associated with Joseph without risk of popular uprising. He takes action – Joseph shall marry the daughter of

Potiphera, priest of Anu in the city of On. Joseph shall become ritually clean, and all Egypt shall know it.

Joseph is told. He has seen the girl once. Her name is Asenath. She is like a young, copper-coloured grasshopper, so slight of frame as to be inconsequential. She did not glide serenely as Egyptian maidens should. She either hopped and flitted, or lowered her brow, digging in her heels. She had not yet blossomed, but Joseph knew that in a year's time she would. Egyptians bloom quickly. He liked her because she seemed an outsider to the decorum of the palace. He remembers the butterfly's light touch, the kindness of insects.

Joseph assents. But he is not joyous. He has become like Esau, marrying a foreign woman. He feels the knife his brothers had meant for him sever completely his link to his bloodline.

The Nile floods four more times, seven times in all since he became vizier. Joseph looks back and sees that the decision to marry was right. He is no longer alone. He can begin to forget his sorrow. Before the years of famine come, his wife, Asenath – named for her goddess, Neith – bears his first son, Manasseh ('making to forget'). The infant is so named because Joseph can now truly say: God has made me forget all the hardship and all my father's house. Joseph has made his decision. His internal tribal court is silenced, and his distress is lessened.

The birth of his second son does not kill his wife, his lovely spirited grasshopper. There is no return of that childhood cataclysm. Now Joseph begins to feel a fullness of joy, like a river in flood. His fears fade. He names the boy Ephraim, 'for God has made me fruitful in the land of my misfortunes'.

Joseph, now named Zapheneth-paneah, inhabits fully his above-ground life. He has left his kin. His skill as vizier grows and he fills the space he commands. He has come into Egypt.

4

River in Drought

Forgiveness and unforgiveness

———•◆•———

The wind changes. A smell of rotting fish is dragged up with the rising sun. For the second year the banks of the Nile are exposed like old flesh. Goats roam the irrigation channels scavenging dry grass. The grain dies on the stalk. Osiris dies, but he does not rise. The sacred lake before the temple is dry. Ma'at is disrupted.

The people are panicking. They cry and beseech Pharaoh, desperate for grain. The divine order of the kingdom trembles on every parched stalk. Pharaoh says: Go to Joseph; do what he says to you to do. To himself he thinks: Let him fix it, let him bear the brunt. Ma'at is depleted and sad, I must make her happy and restore her with offerings.

Drought continues to spread across the whole land of Egypt. Joseph has known it was coming. He could smell the change: no more sweet damp Nile air to intoxicate him morning and evening. Instead, there are more frogs. More insects. The air is thick with their drumming and sticky with decay.

The famine spreads further, to the ends of the earth. Hearing that Egypt has stores of grain, all the world comes to buy bread. Hebrews also come to the land.

Joseph returns from his chariot journeys throughout Egypt – opening the temple storehouses in all the cities, selling grain to the people. A cry goes up; it seems louder than others – 'Habirus, Habirus'. Thus he hears of the arrival of Hebrews, and stumbles.

The earth opens up. The prison swallows him. His pounding heart and sweating palms are those of a sixteen-year-old, bound hand and foot at the bottom of a pit. Breathing fast, tunnel-visioned, Joseph scans the corridor for danger. He races to his quarters, but his breathing won't work, and he tumbles down the steps into his chamber, papyrus scrolls flying. Quickly – lest the servants hear and attend – his free hand flies up to catch the scrolls before their casements clank on the stone floor. Oath – one foot slips. His vizier's headdress leaps off his head, catapults off his reaching fingertips, hits the brazier and cartwheels across the floor.

Joseph looks at the oddly shaped hat, pointed at one end, now lying dented on the floor. A foreign thing. His ears are suddenly opened, and the thunder discharged by a host of bloated, belching frogs invades the room. The mockery! Joseph has been deaf to their raucous humour, all these months laughing at him in his funny hat. The insects whirr in confirmation. He too wants to laugh, but finds his eyes are crying.

He is young Joseph again, surrounded by his tribe, the Hebrews. He knows that he is simply Joseph, the below-ground boy posturing in this strange place, surrounded by danger. The cataclysm has returned.

No one must know this. He replaces the vizier's crown upon his head, perfecting its position. He composes himself with the headdress ritual. He needs this hat, this guise, to face down the terror. He corrects his eye-paint, and straightens his golden collar. He marches out to confront the unknown Hebrews, who are a dusty, famished, exhausted lot.

Out of an indistinct mass emerge ten brothers. Their smell of sweat, wool and goatskin awakens in Joseph the tent, the longing. His senses are drowning before his heart can understand.

The brothers come to him and bow down before him, their faces to the ground. The deafening shock that has opened his ears now opens his eyes. He recognizes them. But he can see that his ten brothers do not recognize him. He distances them with harsh words, speaking only through an interpreter. His dreams have finally come true. But they are not the dreams he wanted.

Joseph demands	Where do you come from?
One of the brothers	From the land of Canaan, to buy food.
Joseph	You are spies; you have come to see the nakedness of the land!
One of the brothers	No, my lord. We are all sons of one man; we are honest men; your servants have never been spies.
Joseph	No, you are spies; you have come to see the nakedness of the land!
One of the brothers	We your servants are twelve brothers, the sons of a certain man in the land of Canaan; the youngest however is with our father, and one brother is no more.
Joseph	It is just as I have said; you are spies. You shall be tested: as Pharaoh lives, you are spies.

Joseph throws them into prison for three days. The liars. He hates them all. But more, he wishes they had loved him. His heart is a dark turmoil. He must think. If each of his heart's thoughts could be rolled out on a long scroll, perhaps he could find the path of wisdom. But now, all is storm.

This is an age when wrongs are righted by punishment. In Egypt, for lesser crimes – beatings, mutilation, fines; for major crimes – death. Hit back hard; no other option. The essential task for ancient societies is the maintenance of order. At all costs, keep the chaos of famine, invasion or nomadic hordes at bay. Uphold the divine rule of the king, or suffer for the affront to the sacred order. The choice is black or white. This is the rule of Egypt.

The rule of nomadic existence was no less harsh. 'An eye for an eye, a tooth for a tooth' is a much later moral advance – it limits revenge to exacting repayments merely proportional to the loss. While minor affronts between tribal members might be resolved by face-saving appeasement, serious crimes required punishment meted out by the tribal powers. At this point in history, the idea of radical, no-strings-attached forgiveness is only gestating; Joseph's story is one of humanity's earliest glimmerings of it.

Joseph is buying time. What should he do? It is his task as vizier to maintain order, to punish infractions. And he has *reasons*. But he finds himself stalling over the three days, buying time, improvising in uncharted territory.

Forgiveness, in any era, is against the odds. We are easily dissuaded from it; almost any excuse will suffice. Psychologists Everett Worthington, Liz Gulliford and others have recently focused on forgiveness, and found it to be vital for psychological healing. The realm of religious insight has finally entered the counselling room, perhaps long overdue. To be able to forgive can be an agonizing labour, but it offers the prize of freeing us from those who have hurt us.

Forgiveness can flow suddenly, or dam up along the way. Some are swept by its force, and find they forgive almost instantly. But for many people, forgiveness is long, slow work. To even start the process, a person who has been harmed needs to acknowledge that a wrong has been committed. This may seem obvious. But we often want to deny what has hurt us, to wave it away in order to leap to a 'Christian' forgiveness: Oh, it doesn't really matter.

Joseph knows he had been wronged. His face is a frozen mask while his thoughts churn: It is as you liars say, one brother is no more. Not by accident. You tried to kill him. You betrayed him. You took away his former life. That brother of yours has suffered for over half his life because of you. This cannot be undone. It cannot forgotten, or swept aside.

To acknowledge the wrong is to disentangle the self from the affliction it has swallowed. The humiliation and rejection finalized in public. The shame of it tasted in private. There is a need to isolate the offence so that the self is no longer swallowed by it, no longer demeaned or destroyed by it. But who can bear witness to this process, to help Joseph separate himself from the shame and wrong he has been forced to internalize?

A witness is needed. Our true identity is strengthened when our deep feelings are mirrored back by someone who stands with us, and feels with us what we are suffering. What we feel deep down becomes more real, more present to us, if someone can truly hear us. A river of emotions can then unblock: fear, anger, hurt, rage, sadness, bitterness, hopelessness, self-condemnation. What has been dammed up must flow.

Sometimes well-meaning religious people try to deflect a hurt person from experiencing their pain and rage, to hurry them towards a forgiveness that sweeps it under the carpet. Yes, there is evidence that continual rumination on negative feelings can prolong depression and anger, but there is also evidence that unless we own our deep feelings, and find a safe way to express them, those feelings can own us. Some people say you have to *forget* in order to forgive. This is simply not true. Anything important that has happened to us as human beings we will remember, at some level. God does not *erase* the past – but it can be transformed. And the memory, while not disappearing, may become less painful.

There is a fine line between acknowledging the pain, and wallowing in it. Joseph had no neutral third person to help him name and isolate the wrong, and to disentangle himself from it. It seems Joseph had no safe person to whom he could articulate his heart, in the way we can today – to a good friend or counsellor – in our more psychologically aware age. For any would-be forgiver, there is a need to put the wrong firmly into the past, otherwise unforgiveness, and its continual rumination, keeps the body on high alert to fight back or flee from the danger of the offender harming once again. To Joseph the crucial question is: Is my brothers' offence truly in the past? Or will they do it again? It is hard to disentangle past and present when trapped alone in the tumult of powerful feelings.

Even under ideal conditions, forgiveness cannot be forced, or required. It may start as a small trickle, uncertain, mixed with sludge. It may be necessary to put in place impediments against further abuse: No, I won't allow that any more. In some cases it might mean removing yourself from a harmful relationship. Forgiving does not mean being a martyr and allowing ongoing damage. Forgiveness is not about tolerating abuse in order to finally 'get this person to love me'. The offence must be realistically in the past. We need to be safe from further abuse in *order* to forgive. Even then, it is a tug of war. In the eyes of justice, the hurt person has the right to recompense. Retribution against the offender would be justified.

Joseph has the right to exact justice – and the power. He contemplates this while his brothers are in prison. Is he not giving them a taste of their own medicine? Let them suffer. Let them feel what it was like.

Joseph is also feeling what it is like for *them*. He remembers well his own paralysing terror, sitting in a foreign prison, surrounded by a strange, ugly language. With this glimmer of fellow-feeling, forgiveness gathers momentum. There comes a point when the offended person begins to make a decision – a decision *not* to exact retribution or seek recompense. To creatively build upon justice, not ignoring it, but going beyond it. Empathy, feeling for the offender as a fellow human, sparks that decision.

Perhaps Joseph is also wondering if retribution can ever put right the wrong. What good would it do for all ten brothers to rot in prison for ever? Perhaps he recognizes that repaying with violence only compounds sin. Violence upon violence, so common in this age of empires – punishing all enemies, wreaking despair upon all.

On the other hand, is it acceptable to simply wave away the offence? Will not a soft forgiveness invite more wrongdoing, itself becoming an immoral act? Chaos again unleashed? What if Zapheneth-paneah the vizier is seen to be deficient in his exercise of legal rule?

Two opposing moral values are in dynamic tension here: the need for justice versus a desire for restored relationship. Both are important. Both need to be weighed in the balance. To forgive is to hold these two values in a complex moral balancing act.

Joseph finds he refuses to simply destroy his brothers. Yes, he wants justice, and yet he wants his brothers too. Their fate is in his hands. Only Joseph can make the free gift of forgiveness to his brothers. Only the offended can forgive the offender. Joseph is the fulcrum. It hangs on him to make this decision, no one else. Forgiveness does not depend on how sorry the offenders are – those lying brothers of his. It does not depend on whether the offence can be turned around. Joseph knows that he has been permanently altered by their actions – even his Egyptian name Zapheneth-paneah is a foreign-sounding thing.

He is contemplating something so novel that even the scribes do not have a picture-word to describe it. Yes, he knows well the tribal rules for appeasement, when both parties settle an old score. Rules for buying back favour, saving face, avoiding endless tribal vendettas. I'll give you this payment for that stolen goat. I will appease your honour so that you do not lose face, just as his father, Jacob, strengthened by the angel, was able to appease his brother, Esau, with lavish gifts, buying his pardon and release from retribution. But what Joseph is contemplating is something more radical. It does not wait for an apology; this may never be forthcoming. Forgiveness grabs reality by the neck, looks it in the face, and decides what to do – to let the guilty go free. It is a choice that depends on nothing except the forgiver, and the forgiver being able, realistically, to put the offence into the past. For Joseph, it is a new reality dawning, a flickering light, yet unnamed.

We moderns are still figuring it out. Recent research and clinical experience clarify the stages of forgiveness into models described by psychologists Robert D. Enright, Suzanne Freedman and Julio Rique, and similarly by Everett Worthington:

1 *The uncovering phase* involves facing the hurt and shame caused by the offence, facing up to the possibility of being permanently changed by the offence. We may have to face that the world is not as just or fair as we previously thought, that bad things can happen to good people.

2 *The decision phase* heralds a change of heart. Perhaps the old strategies of resentment or anger are simply not working. We begin with a willingness to forgive. This needs to be sealed by a commitment to forgive. And returned to again and again, as the forgiveness can slide into unforgiveness when we feel the hurt again. We need to reaffirm our commitment to forgive.

3 Now the *work phase* begins. Deliberate effort is required to move more deeply into forgiveness. We have to work on our thoughts and our feelings about the offender. Our thinking

may have become constricted and biased; we see the offender as 'all bad'. We may need to revise how we see that person. We may need to develop empathy for them, and even consider what suffering the offender might be experiencing, in his guilt and alienation. To do any of this, we need to have accepted our own woundedness, which means we need to see ourselves compassionately – as a mother would see her own child.

4 Finally a *deepening phase* involves finding meaning as the hurt is transformed into effective action to protect others, or into compassion for those who have suffered like us. We come to realize that all human beings – offenders and offended – need mercy and compassion. As we realize we are not alone in our struggle, negative feelings begin to decrease; some positive feelings for the offender may become possible. We begin to feel free.

It is easy to get stuck. Anger and resentment keep coming back. Unforgiveness does not mean no progress has been made, but it does mean that we have to keep on working at it. We have to keep returning to the commitment we made to forgive. A strategy in the *work phase* that enables forgiveness to deepen is to *reframe* a person's wrongdoing. That means we try to see what motivated them, what context in their life contributed to their wrongdoing. It doesn't mean we condone what they have done, but we put ourselves in their shoes and try to see the world from their perspective. Perhaps, realistically, that person is *unable* to behave in the way we would hope. Reframing asks: Has the person who has victimized me been a victim himself or herself? As the psychologist Karl Menninger famously said: We are all victims of victims. We grow to see that the offender is not a complete monster – but, like ourselves, is a hurt person blind about their hurtfulness.

But reframing may not work in all situations. What if the more we try to see why a person did this to us, the more obscene the offence becomes? Victims of holocausts and ethnic cleansings, forced to witness the torture and murder of their kin, may never be able to convincingly reframe what was done. Some offences are beyond human understanding. But in some situations, reframing can be a useful step in forgiving. It represents an attempt to separate the sinner from the sin, to get rid of some of our usual biases in how we view offenders – as 'totally evil'. Doing this, we begin to see them in a more complex, realistic way, bringing them down to size.

Another strategy is *empathy* – to put oneself in the place of the offender. This seems a risky step – to empathize not just with our own or other victims' pain, but to imagine the way the offender is feeling about what they have done. To feel for them in their guilt, alienation and darkness, even if they are outwardly denying it. Our heart moves towards the offender. Or, we imagine God's heart moving towards the offender. Research shows this movement of heart towards the offender is the most crucial step in the journey of forgiveness. The battle is won through empathy.

However, there may be huge obstacles against feeling empathy for an offender, especially if the offender has behaved in a grotesque way. We may be too damaged, our sense of self destroyed by what the offender has done. We may be too outraged to feel anything for the offender. No one should require a devastated person to rise to heroics beyond them.

So, another strategy can be tried: the *role-taking* approach. In life, we all assume roles. Joseph puts on the role of vizier, and he grows into the role over time. Similarly, the role of forgiver may be grown into over time. This can free us from the huge task of forgiving everything at a stroke. It enables us to redefine ourselves, inch by inch, as forgivers. By practising the actions of forgiveness, we can gradually lay down the burden of resentment. Is it false to play the role of forgiver? Not if we understand that forgiveness is a process, and that gradually our feelings may be brought into line.

How we motivate ourselves to move past our own barriers of rage and pain is up to the individual. We can try out reframing what happened in the past, or empathizing with how the offender is feeling in the present, or imagining what life might be like in the future if we could begin to forgive. A better future can draw us towards its light.

Even if the relationship remains unreconciled, forgiveness is a good outcome. We aren't expecting anything more from that person. We aren't tied to them any more. In that sense we are free to get on with living. It may not be safe or realistic to clutch them to our bosom in an intimate relationship. But we no longer wish them harm. We are free to wish them good. We may even be able to cease avoiding them. The door is kept open – maybe one day the relationship will be fully repaired, on both sides. But we don't expect them to meet our need.

Joseph's story, with its intricate detail here, fits well with complexities of forgiveness as a process that takes time. The process may zig and zag, one step forwards, two steps back. It can get stuck, and then restart. At this point in the narrative, Joseph's motives seem mixed.

At one level, he is messing with his brothers' heads. He is confusing them, frightening them and forcing them to experience the terror and degradation he imbibed for so long. He is paying them back, at least in part. He may be testing himself, seeing how he feels about what he is doing to them. He seems also to be educating their moral sense, so that they will know what it feels like to be helpless and terrified. Perhaps in the future they will feel more empathy, and become more compassionate. By shaping their moral sense, he may also be making himself safe from further abuse, thus putting their offence into the past. He also seems to be trying to gauge whether relationship with his brothers is now possible. He isn't satisfied simply to 'move on with his life'. He desires reconciliation with his brothers. He is looking for a way in, to see if they have changed.

While forgiveness requires nothing in response from the offender, reconciliation does. Reconciliation works only when both parties move towards each other in honesty and trust. Will his brothers face up to what they have done, or continue in denial and falsehood? Joseph seems to be aiming for a truthful reconciliation that builds on the free gift of forgiveness.

Joseph is shaped by the collective cultures of the ancient Middle East: a person is defined by their family relationships. In that context a person lived, loved and died. Our individualistic milieu contents us to walk away from broken relationships. Not so for Joseph, a true Hebrew. Similarly, Christian forgiveness strives to be reconciled, if that is at all possible. The onus is on us, whether offended or offender, to try to restore the relationship. If your brother has something against you, leave your gift at the altar and go to him to be reconciled, exhorts the writer of Matthew's Gospel. St Paul says, with a note of realism: As far as it is possible with you, live at peace with all.

After three days' imprisonment, Joseph says to his brothers:

> Do this and you shall live, for I fear God: if you are honest men, let one of your brothers stay here where you are imprisoned. The rest of you shall go to Canaan and carry grain for the famine of your households. Bring back your youngest brother to me. Thus your words will be verified, and you shall not die.

The brothers agree. They say to one another: We are paying the penalty for what we did to Joseph; we saw his anguish when he pleaded with us, but we would not listen. That is why this anguish has come upon us.

Then Reuben, as always inflating his innocence, says: Did I not tell you not to wrong the boy? But you would not listen. So now comes a reckoning for his blood.

They do not know that Joseph understands what they are saying. Joseph turns away from them, moves to the window and weeps, focusing on the parched land before him. The dry vista seems to him the very scene of the events his brothers describe. But in public they continue to deny it. The knife twists; Joseph's heart drains away its small hope. He reforms himself back into the vizier, and turns back to them. He picks out Simeon and has him bound before their eyes.

How closely did he recreate his own cataclysm for them? Did he have Simeon tripped, and have his face pressed into the jagged dry ground, elbows trussed behind his back so tightly that they are cut off from his body, his limbs forced to join those asleep in Sheol? Did he have Simeon thrown into the pit for the waiting buzzards?

The other brothers are free to leave: Return to Canaan, bring with you as much grain as you can carry. Joseph gives orders to the servants to fill the brothers' bags with grain, and to give them provisions for their journey, and – double-cross – to return every man's money to his sack.

The nine brothers load their donkeys and depart, leaving Simeon bound in Egypt. Their loads are heavy with familiar guilt. Their journey is silent. Later, at the lodging place, one brother opens his sack to give his donkey fodder, and sees his money at the top of his sack. He cries out in despair. At this they lose heart. They turn trembling to one another: What is this that God has done to us?

Too soon they cross the wilderness and come to their father, Jacob, in Canaan, who is anxiously awaiting their return. They tell him all that happened, while erecting a buffer against the real meaning of the events. Jacob, who had forbidden them to take young Benjamin to Egypt with them for this very reason, bewails: And now Simeon is lost.

They try to explain to Jacob that the vizier insisted: By this shall I know that you are honest men – leave one of your brothers with me, take grain for the famine, and go your way. Bring your youngest brother to me, and I shall know that you are not spies but honest men. Then I will release your brother Simeon to you, and you may trade in the land.

Jacob cries out	I am the one you have bereaved of children; Joseph is no more, and Simeon is no more, and now you would take Benjamin. All this has happened to *me*!
Reuben says	You may kill my two sons if I do not bring him back to you. Put him in my hands.
But Jacob will not	If harm should come to Benjamin on the journey to Egypt, you will bring down my grey hairs to Sheol.
	They cannot think. They stall, busy themselves, avoid, until the family has eaten all the grain. The famine continues unabated.
Defeated, Jacob finally says	Go down to Egypt, and buy more food.
Judah reminds him	The man solemnly warned us: 'You shall not see my face unless your youngest brother is with you.'
Jacob cries	Why did you treat me so badly as to tell the man you had another brother?
Judah argues	The man questioned us carefully, saying: 'Is your father alive? Have you another brother?' What we told him was in answer to these questions. Could we have known that he would say: 'Bring your youngest

brother down'? Send Benjamin with me, let us be on our way so that we may live and not die – you and we and all our little ones. I myself will be surety for him; you can hold me accountable for him. If I do not bring him back to you . . . then let me bear the blame for ever.

Jacob replies   If it must be so, then do this . . . take gifts, balm, honey, gum, resin, pistachios and almonds, take back double the money. Perhaps the money in your sacks was an oversight. Take your youngest brother Benjamin also . . . As for me, I am bereaved. I am bereaved.

While the brothers are away, Joseph lives Simeon's incarceration. Each day he wanders the halls of Pharaoh's palace and its adjacent prison corridors. He paces now as he did formerly, four strides back and forth, across the narrow space. He studies the corridor's wall carvings, its vivid colours – gold ochre, turquoise and red, outlined in charcoal black, flickering in the torchlight. He examines the images of scores of prisoners bowing before Pharaoh, the king's arm holding his crook across his chest, his fist with its flail raised in triumph, riding his chariot over the bodies of the headless defeated.

Enemies will face their allotted end. Then comes the journey to the land of the dead, and the judgement before the gods. The journey is prepared. The soul, the *ba*, and the soul's energy, the *ka*, are transported by sacred barge across the dark river. Jackal-headed Anubis is waiting, always waiting. The flames shift and flutter. A gust of wind. A torch blows out, like the life of the body. In the half-light, the pantheon of the gods, Amun-Ra at its head, falcon-headed Horus next, all come to bear witness.

The god Seth appears; his task is to impose the dismemberment of death, the isolation and chaos of death. The soul's disembodied heart is taken and weighed before Osiris, the judge of the underworld, weighed on the scales against Ma'at's feather of truth. Anubis and Horus stand at either side of the soul's *ba*. There is no chance the verdict will miscarry. All the gods are present; together they know all this life has entailed. Thoth, god of the scribes, records the judgement, finalizing it for all eternity.

Joseph tastes the knowledge that his heart is mixed, of substances both heavy and light. The wall paintings sift him as chaff from wheat. If he died now, would Osiris allow him to live again? Would his energy be allowed to find anchor in his bodily remains, or would it be expelled for ever, to wander without home? Will his body's entrails be protected by Horus' four sons against the second death that erases the soul? What does the Book of the Dead proclaim? A metallic taste of dread floods him. He knows he would fail the judgement.

He must get out. His breath is trapped. He retraces his steps, looking for the way out. He hits a dead end, forces the stone, it refuses to shift. He forces it again . . . immoveable . . . he runs . . . the other corridor is a dead end too. He turns to the right, then runs down the left, the prison corridors are all the same. Torches gutter and fight to stay alight. He starts to panic. His hatred of closed spaces, the dark, the dank, the eternity of imprisonment. Those who know the secret corridors to the burial chamber – on the day of Pharaoh's funeral – will themselves remain buried alive as the vast entrance stones descend while the supporting sand escapes, trapped by the impenetrable barrier engineered against grave robbers. Pharaoh's treasures, gilded for his eternal journey, are protected for ever as the stones come crashing down. A sickening revolt twists Joseph's stomach. His heart's walls are caving in, carved with his nail marks like the walls of pit and prison.

More than life itself, Joseph wants escape. Air and light. He must have air. He vows to release his brothers from this fate – if only he can find his way out. May the gods help him. May the Elohim of his father help him. He tries another corridor – the endless, frustrating maze. Spirits of prisoners, their *ka*, their *ba*, all the defeated, confusing him with their cacophony of cries.

A shadow halts his progress. Time stops. He cannot move, he cannot breathe. The shadow will not release him; it will not release his brothers. No one shall move from here. Justice requires punishment. The order of the realm is immutable. Written. Release them, let them live? No. It does not wish to.

The onyx shadow touches him, a chill breeze. Joseph is crippled by the fear of it. The 'it' is faceless – immeasurably tall, knife-pointed, a dark obelisk, cruel as triumph. Joseph's *ba* and *ka* give up. The torch behind him intensifies and blazes, and the shadow jumps toward the wall, just as he jumps.

Pressed against the wall, he now sees. The shadow is himself. The vizier.

5

River in Flood

Loss and grieving

———◆◆◆———

Rising from a dreamless sleep, Joseph feels his recent panic fade away. Those events are hazy now. What was he doing wandering those prison corridors?

A kindly morning light slips over the horizon, touching the hem of the temple. He watches as the stone rams, the very image of Ra, absorb the melon hue of dawn. A scattering of birds sings of survival: We are here, we are here. The sun god Ra still reigns, despite the frogs and the stench of mud.

No need to fear. His dreams are proving true. There will be seven years of drought. Two such years have already passed. His solemn task is to ensure survival for the whole land of Egypt. As vizier, he is invested with the power to store grain, to sell it, to organize and distribute it, to write down to whom it is sold, and how much remains in the temple storehouses in Memph, Thebes, or Edfu. This act of writing has a strange power, he discovers. Writing makes his pronouncements more permanent, his words more lasting. His picture-words now exist in another realm, where no one can contradict them. Even the flowing, cursive writing used by scribes creates words that will last for ever, like temples to the gods.

Joseph wields this writing power now. He thinks of his brothers, who lack this power. And of Simeon, still in prison. He has been there once himself, for a long time. At the bottom, crushed by the vast pyramid of power above him. Now that he is at the top of the pyramid, why should he suffer a reversal of the appointed order? Why should he let his brothers live without punishment? He will not think about his brothers.

He is beginning to understand the world as seen by the Egyptians. He sees that the gods of Egypt live in the unchanging realm of picture-words, this realm recorded by scribes, immortalized in friezes in temples and tombs. In this eternal realm, each god commands its own forces, its own domain: the power of the sun, the life-giving force of the Nile, the mysteries of night, grain, childbirth, death, chaos, justice and rebirth. These powers enable life to unfurl in Egypt, in all its joy, all its struggle, and to continue in the afterlife amidst sun-blessed green fields. This mesh of interlinking gods, he now understands, needs to be refreshed with offerings, lest any of the gods becomes depleted, tipping the delicate balance between gods, humans and animals, as has happened in this drought, and long ago – disastrously ending former dynasties.

It is so clear to him now. He understands that the great loom of Ma'at needs to be interwoven with harmonious human relationships: families, labourers, artisans, lords, priests, priestesses, vizier and Pharaoh, all sustaining the pyramid of power, the appointed order. All must make offerings. Most of all, Pharaoh, the living embodiment of falcon-faced Horus, Lord of the Sky, must provide the right offerings. Joseph understands this now. The life he experiences in Egypt makes sense when seen through this delicately balanced loom of power.

At night, he remembers his father's stories. They are written on his heart as upon granite. He will not allow them to be erased – not as obelisks are erased when a new dynasty erupts. His stories are always there. Of late, he has been telling his father's stories to the Egyptians. Even Pharaoh listens. They seem odd stories to them, but the people of the land are so religious that they are eager to learn about a different god. They are curious about the unseen Elohim who has no image, who rules in Canaan among the Habirus. They do not understand how to listen to these small, ordinary stories. These stories, Joseph feels, make sense not just by hearing them, but by living them, testing them out against life events, as they have been experienced by Jacob's small tribe for three generations. They are not written down; they are lived. The Hebrews have no scribes. Hearing this, the Egyptians look at each other, aghast.

But, Joseph cannot think of those stories now. Only the exercise of his power will make Egypt safe. He must make it safe. If he demurs, chaos will be unleashed. As vizier, he cannot loosen his grip. He cannot open the boundaries of the land to spies. He cannot let prisoners go free. Joseph knows that if he removes his headdress, and all it stands for, he exposes not only the land but also himself to threat. He needs this protection. He cannot dismantle the tall shadow he encountered in the stone corridor. He cannot attack it, or outsmart it. The business of the kingdom must proceed as is. He will attend to his duties.

He commands Asenath: Tell the servants to prepare a banquet. His wife tilts her head and looks up at him. Her right foot twists back and forth on its narrow ankle, her way of biding time. He has seen this before. She purses her lips, folds her arms, and breathes out a long sigh. Her smile starts to break through her attempted frown. Just like this morning's play of light.

His son Manasseh, now three years old, catches her mood of resistance, and hurls a playful kick at her shin. Like lightning, she catches his wrist, and draws his face close to hers. She opens wide her eyes at him, brows raised, making the scary mask – the one he adores. Manasseh squirms with delight and whoops into laughter. He somersaults in reply. He turns his face upside-down, and looks up at her from between his legs, making the scary mask. Her turn to laugh.

78

Young Ephraim, not to be outshone, toddles in, his speeding legs unpractised but ever hopeful. His brother's mirror, Ephraim turns himself upside-down. Look, I can do it! But his balance is yet unborn, and he falls over in slow motion, bottom first, with a discernible bounce. Joseph's laugh breaks out – a crane arising from the reeds. His family – the endless pageant that they are.

His heart suddenly commands him: Invite your brothers! Give the banquet for them! He has heard that the brothers had returned once again to the land. His longing for them is again unleashed. It is stronger than justice.

Asenath studies him. She lifts her two palms to him, making the graceful blessing given to husband and to gods. This ritual performed, she tilts her head the other way, eyes rolled, and makes the sound 'N', which in the Egyptian tongue means: Read this in the negative. And laughs. She turns on her heel. The imp. She should be renamed 'the mischievous one'. He can read her intentions from across the room.

Joseph laughs even louder as he strides down the hall, shouting back to her: Double portions! Give them all double portions!

The river inside him begins to flow. Surprised at himself, and his adamant reversal, he hurries to ensure the preparations. He watches as the servant slaughters the animal for the feast, the blood gushing red from the swift cut. He sends out a runner to invite his brothers, to bring them back to his house. He misses them. In his excitement he shouts: Prepare figs, dates, honeyed wine, grapes, squash, leeks, and slather the garlic on the meat! Some hours later, Joseph's steward greets the brothers at the entrance.

The ten brothers are terrified, and are certain of their thinking: We have been brought here because of the silver that was put into our sacks the first time. He wants to overpower us and seize us as slaves and take our donkeys.

They make their case to the steward:

> Please sir, we came down here the first time to buy food. But at
> the place where we stopped for the night we opened our sacks
> and each one of us found his silver – the exact weight – in the
> mouth of his sack. So we have brought it back with us. We have
> also brought additional silver with us to buy food. We don't
> know who put the silver in our sacks.

The steward, knowing Joseph well, tells them: It is all right.
Your God, the God of your fathers, has given you treasure in
your sacks; I received your silver.

It is late morning. Simeon is released from prison and brought
out to them. Alive, safe, free. The sun shines brightly upon
their good fortune, their embraces and their shouts in the
still cool, late-morning air. Quiet, hush, don't reveal too much.
They smooth Simeon's rough garments, his unruly hair.
They test the thinness of his shoulders, yes, he is still healthy,
he is still alive. Judah thinks of his little ones; they are now
safe. This day is a good day for them, though everything is
upside-down and unexpected. Judah almost dares to hope.
The brothers are brought into the vizier's chambers. They are
given water to wash their feet; there is fodder for their donkeys.
The banquet will be at noon. The air is dry and clear in the
bright sun.

Inside the house, they stand gazing upwards at the smooth
ceilings, then down to the cool polished floors. Astonished,
they watch small feline creatures meander and massage themselves against the bronze legs of couches, calm as lords. Their
rhythmic effect is echoed by the ochre, green and red figures
on the walls. Servant women, with bare arms covered only with
protective amulets, glide past them.

The vizier strides in. The brothers bow down, and lay before
him the gifts they have brought from Canaan. He asks them:

How is your aged father you told me about? Is he still living? They answer: Your servant our father is alive and well. They bow down again to pay him honour.

Joseph looks about him and asks: Is this your youngest brother, the one you told me about? He sees Benjamin clearly for the first time, as his full brother, his own mother's son, steps forward. This face, so singular, could belong to no other.

Joseph drinks in the features familiar yet foreign now to his Egypt-accustomed eyes. He moves closer to study his brother. Benjamin's thick curls lift off his high forehead with a life of their own, dark as night, burnished with red where the sun strikes them. The hair falls to his shoulders in regular, horizontal waves, separating at the ends into untamed curls – not woven straight like the blunt-shaped wigs of Egypt. Alive. The hair is shiny, perhaps oiled, glinting like a campfire at night. Impressive, strong hair. His face is unlined. He is still young. His neck is long, sturdy like a pillar.

Benjamin's skin is not Egyptian. It is not the skin of a serene, benign mask, coated with the fine dust that blows off the desert. This skin is mobile, pale where not burned by the sun, with distinct pores – damp, and alive with emotion. An uncertain smile quivers, curling up at one end. His eyebrows leap upwards as if forming a question. This skin reflects, changing its cast from moment to moment.

Joseph studies Benjamin's large, almond eyes – so clear, the whites like milk. He can make out each individual charcoal lash curling upwards, long and sweeping. Benjamin's eyes are not dark. They are a surprise – they are light silver-grey like well-water, like the stone called agate. Yet they flash with gold, fiery as a brazier's flame. Both cool and warm. Eyes that mirror his own. A face glimpsed at the bottom of a well.

In a choked voice, Joseph whispers: God be gracious to you, my son. Joseph rushes out and looks for a place to weep.

He washes his face and composes himself. He replaces his headdress with the familiar ritual. Controlling himself, he uses the Egyptian tongue as he commands: Serve the food.

He looks about and now takes in each of his brothers' faces. He had not really *seen* them earlier. Before, his brothers were a mass, a horde. Now, he can see each one. Each face, so different from the others, yet unlike the faces of any other tribe. Reuben and Judah, tall, with their imposing shoulders, their powerful hands, their dark eyes flashing from skin now creased with lines, their strong features, a sense of urgency in every move. Reuben's beard long and undulating, Judah's beard dense and curled. Zebulun, of slighter frame, with a sweet calm face; he could be an Egyptian. Issachar and Asher, sturdy, with black eyes like Jacob's. Gad, tall and thin, wiry hair coiled in the tightest of curls. Naphtali, like Judah in features, but with Zebulun's lighter frame. Each face uniquely carved, each one painted according to its own form of beauty. Simeon, exuding joy and relief, his curling hair the soft colour of sand. Joseph is drawn again to the light eyes of Benjamin, both warm and cool, like his own.

Protocol must be observed. The brothers are seated in order, from firstborn to the youngest. The attendants serve the vizier by himself, and his brothers separately. The invited Egyptians eat by themselves because it is detestable for them to eat with Hebrews, from whom they catch a whiff of animal, sweat and wool.

The brothers look at each other in astonishment. The huge portions. The roasted meat! The wine. The dates and figs. They feast and drink freely, their hearts unloaded like heavy packs. Benjamin is served a portion five times greater than anyone else. But no one minds. Their joy is a tumult.

At the end of the banquet Joseph quietly commands the steward: Fill the men's sacks with as much grain as they can carry, and put each man's silver in the mouth of his sack. Then put my cup, the silver one, in the sack of the youngest, along with the silver for his grain.

The brothers depart for Canaan, their donkeys laden, their stomachs full. Their jubilation fades to a soft sound, their bells tinkling in the distance. When they are well out of the city, where the stone mansions cease and the thatched, mud-brick huts of labourers begin, Joseph tells his steward to go after them, catch up with them and demand: Why did you return good with evil? Isn't this the cup my master drinks from and uses for divination? This is a wicked thing you have done.

When the steward catches up with the brothers, they are shocked and dismayed, their voices rising high like women's, hands flailing, feet stamping:

> Why does my lord say such things? Far be it from your servants to do anything like that! We even brought back to you from Canaan the silver we found inside our sacks. So why would we steal silver or gold from your master's house? If any of your servants is found to have it, he will die; and the rest of us will become your slaves.

Lessening the extremity of their oaths, the steward replies: Very well, whoever is found to have it will become my slave. The rest of you will be free from blame.

They lay open their sacks, and the steward begins the search, beginning with the oldest, ending with the youngest. They find the goblet in Benjamin's sack. It glows brazenly, its bowl peeking above the dusty grain. At this sight, they all tear their clothes. They replace their sacks upon their animals, a moment ever repeating itself, stolen from a nightmare.

They journey back, nearly lame with the fear of guilt, and re-enter the vizier's house. Judah and his brothers throw themselves before Joseph.

Joseph says to them	What have you done? Do you not know that a man like me can find things out by divination?
Judah replies in despair	What can we say? How can we prove our innocence? God has uncovered your servants' guilt. We are now my lord's slaves – we ourselves and the one who was found to have the cup.
Joseph, the rule-bearer, replies	Far be it from me to do such a thing. Only the man who was found to have the cup will become my slave. The rest of you, go back to your father in peace.
Judah turns back and approaches the vizier	Please, let your servant speak a word to my lord. Do not be angry with your servant although you are equal to Pharaoh himself. My lord asked his servants, 'Do you have a father or a brother?' And we answered, 'We have an aged father, and there is a young son born to him in his old age. His brother is dead, and he is the only one of his mother's sons, and his father loves him.'
Judah continues	Then you said to your servants, 'Bring him down to me so that I can see him for myself.' And we said to my lord, 'He cannot leave his father; if he leaves his father, his father will die.' But you told your servants, 'Unless your youngest brother comes with you, you will not see my face.' Your servant my father said to me, 'You know that my wife has borne me two sons. One of them went away from me, and I said, "Truly he has been torn to pieces." And I have not seen him since. If you take this one too

from me, you will bring my grey hairs down to the grave in misery.'

Judah says If the boy is not with us when we go back to my father, whose life is bound up with the boy's life, and he sees that the boy isn't there, he will die. Your servant guaranteed the boy's safety to my father: If I do not bring him back to you, I will bear the blame before you, my father, all my life. Please then, let your servant remain here in place of the boy, and let the boy return with his brothers. How can I go back to my father if the boy is not with me? No! Do not let me see the misery that would come upon my father.

Joseph can no longer control himself. The father that Judah evokes, the evidence of change in Judah, is undoing him. He cries out to all his attendants: Leave my presence!

They drop their tasks and vanish. Joseph is alone with his brothers. His weeping breaks out. Joseph's ragged cries escape as from a wounded animal, bounding off walls and down stone corridors – so loud that the Egyptians hear it. Humiliating, but too late to turn back the flood.

The Egyptians, who strive to achieve composure before all else, their faces becalmed, their linen unmarked, take in Joseph's strange sobs with wide eyes. Even Pharaoh will hear of this. Astonished, they exchange knowing smiles, as if to say to each other: We always knew that he was uncivilized. They turn back to their work, secretly feeling for him in their hearts as for a child not yet fully trained.

Joseph says to his brothers: I am Joseph. His Hebrew words rush forth: Is my father still living? The brothers turn to stone.

'Come close to me,' Joseph says. They shuffle forward on limbs made of dry sticks.

> I am your brother Joseph whom you sold into Egypt. And now, do not be distressed, and do not be angry with yourselves for selling me here, because it was to save lives that God sent me ahead of you. For two years now there has been famine, and for five more there will be no ploughing or reaping. But God sent me here to preserve for you a remnant on earth and to save your lives by a great deliverance.

Joseph's own words surprise him. In recent months he has been beginning to see a picture weaving together, strand by strand, but he could not congeal the words except in Hebrew – that it was out of *hesed* – loving-kindness – for the Egyptians, to save them, that he had come into Egypt. He knew this to be true. And now, a second shock, he sees that it was out of this same *hesed* – loving-kindness – that for his brothers and his whole family he had been thrown into pit and prison. In one stroke, in this one vision – the opposites rushing together – he sees the meaning of his suffering, and finds that he wishes to release his brothers from theirs. The deepest truth is that he has longed for them all the while. His dreams have finally come true.

So then, Joseph says:

> It was not you, but God who sent me here. You can see for yourselves, and so can my brother Benjamin, that it is really I who am speaking to you. Tell my father about all the honour that has been accorded to me. Say to him, 'This is what your son Joseph says: "God has made me lord of all Egypt. Come down to me; do not delay. You shall live in the region of Goshen and be near me – your children and grandchildren, your flocks and herds and all you own. I will provide for you there because there are still five years of famine to come."'

And now his weeping breaks into a full, anguished yet joyful flood. He throws himself onto Benjamin's neck, weeps and kisses him. Benjamin, the silent little brother, is also broken open. He weeps and embraces Joseph, his tall, strong brother finally returned to him from the dead.

The fine features of their own mother's face, never forgotten, are present now to both of them, in their warm and cool eyes, their arched brows. Joseph finds he is weeping most profusely for her, for Rachel, for the Face he lost so long ago. He could not weep for her then. The loss was too great, and he was too small. But now he can weep; he is big enough, strong enough to weep for this and all his losses. In this flow of water she has returned to him, because he is becoming like her, willing to suffer as she did, the suffering to which she gave strange voice so long ago. Her cries then enabled Benjamin to come into life, his brother who is here with him now. Rachel is no longer distant, far away in Sheol, but here now, helping Joseph to live as she would live. He kisses all his brothers and weeps over them.

He glimpses this; the God whom he cannot see has enabled him to see these faces, and to regain his own. Benjamin's face is Joseph's mirror, asking questions of him. It is also his answer – it offers back to him his own *ba*, his own *ka*, knitted to his own flesh. At length they are able to speak, quietly, man to man.

It grows late, and Joseph returns to his chambers, shaky and drunk with joy. His legs are unhinged because his heart is so light. He is astonished by the sudden, clumsy, public meeting that occurred between his two selves – his above-ground vizier self, and his below-ground self – a meeting observed by all – as his two selves merged into one Joseph, accompanied by the fanfare of his loud weeping. And now they all know, Egyptians and family alike. He is frightened, thrilled and calm, all in one. He knows that he is safe. And alive. He has been reborn.

More faces greet him. He is captured by Asenath's dark, burnished face, as if for the first time. He cups her small chin in his hands, and traces her high, round, copper-coloured cheeks, her curved forehead and stubborn pout, her laughing eyes – darkest ebony with sunbursts of gold. He takes her hands and notices how her fingertips, so flexible, arch backwards.

He thinks now of the insects – the dragonflies, the beetles, the locusts, the small buzzing flies – his only friends for so many years. He is grateful to them, and promises not to forget them. But now he is surrounded by so many faces, Egyptians and Hebrews – brothers and sisters, all of them.

How odd that he feels grateful to his brothers for launching him on this long journey. It is too much to comprehend. He wishes now only to rest his burning eyes, and to ponder: what confluence – of his father's God and his fellow human beings – managed to unlock the door that he himself had shut.

<hr />

The river in flood, this story teaches us, is the flow of grief that links our *ba* to our *ka*, and roots us to our physical selves – even as we feel the agonizing chasm that separates us from the ones we have lost. We grieve because we are social beings, because our lives are connected to those whom we love. Grieving is the evidence that love is fundamental to our existence, and its loss brings about the end of life as we have known it. We cannot escape this underside of loving.

Because grieving is about love, and our longing for love, it reveals the essence of what it means to be human. It is from this authentic place that a greater grace can flow – a grace that does not originate in us, but seeks its way through us. Joseph's experience is one in which both forgiveness and grieving join forces to heal – to enable a radical wholeness to invade both himself and others – towards a *shalom* that is the culmination of the Bible's sweeping narratives.

Loss of a close, important relationship is so massive that we are unable to traverse it except in small steps. Like forgiveness, grief can get stuck. Indeed they intertwine. For Joseph, the loss imposed by his brothers' offence was bound up in the early loss of his mother. As Joseph zigged and zagged towards forgiving his brothers, so too was his earlier loss reawakened. It is hard to know which process came first: grieving or forgiving. In Joseph, they seem enmeshed. And underneath all our life experience is that wordless, primal memory of birth – unavailable to our conscious minds – our first struggle and expulsion into the strangeness of life. No wonder we shy away from the full frontal blow of grief, and rush into denial or avoidance.

We have to keep retracing our steps, and starting again. It is vital for the infant to form an attachment with his mother or carer as a first step to establishing a basic trust towards others, and towards life itself. The process of attaching goes on throughout life in all our close relationships. And when we are forced to detach, the reaction is intense. How vehemently upset a securely attached young child is when her mother walks out of the room. She cries out in protest. But when the mother comes back into the room after a brief separation, the child reconnects with mother and calm is restored.

The painful process of losing someone to whom we are attached, and protesting against that loss, is the task of grieving. When we are attached to someone, then lose that attachment, we are shocked, disorientated; we search and protest, we are angry. We blame others – and the deceased. Or we blame ourselves and feel guilty and depressed. Grieving is most often associated with loss through death, but there are other kinds of loss: separation, divorce, amputation, serious illness, infertility, miscarriage, unemployment, or even retirement. None of these can be traversed in one simple step. We face a long journey.

According to the research of Elisabeth Kübler-Ross, Colin Murray Parkes and others, the grieving person is likely to experience different emotional states. Individuals will make their own journeys, in their own way, but experience suggests that there are some common features, just as we have seen in Joseph's responses to his losses:

- *Denial*: No, this can't be happening. It isn't happening. Nothing has changed.
- *Yearning/searching*: Where are you? I hear your voice talking to me from Sheol, but when I look, you aren't here.
- *Bargaining*: If only you will let me escape this prison and live, I will release my brothers from theirs.
- *Anger and protest*: Why *me*? What have I done? I hate them all. Let them suffer as I have suffered.
- *Guilt*: What did I do to deserve this? My brothers despise me; I am unworthy of life.
- *Depression*: There is no way back. I am cut off.
- *Acceptance*: I know you've died, and you won't come back; but you are here, part of me. I see you in my brother's face, and in my own.

No one goes through these stages in a methodical, sequential manner. Instead, grieving is a stop–start process where there are two opposite impulses: the wish to cling, to hold on, not to let the change happen; and the need to let go, to loosen the grip, to let the change have taken place and continue to live. The journey swings between these two impulses, zigging and zagging its messy but necessary way forward, towards eventual acceptance and greater maturity.

We may applaud those who are stoic in the face of loss. But grief that is denied or suppressed for long periods can get stuck.

Culture plays a role here. Adults may not know how to talk with bereaved children like Joseph, to help them grieve. So the child gets stuck in an unexpressed loss. Men may try to cope by getting on with everyday life, paying the bills, burying the pain. The grieving gets frozen.

Women often grieve with more expressed emotion, feeling the pain intensely. It is demanding and draining to do this grief work and we help grieving people by standing alongside them while they do it – not minimizing what they are feeling, not trying to make them feel better, but simply being there with them. However, it is also possible for a person to get stuck in expressed grieving too, forever going round and round the pain, refusing to let life begin again. Queen Victoria's personal shrine to Albert revealed an effort to keep everything the way it once was.

Men's and women's different styles of grieving, when extreme, can add new stresses. For example, a couple may grieve in different ways over their child's death. Perhaps the woman is hurt that her husband doesn't appear to feel the pain as acutely. Perhaps the man finds his wife's preoccupation with the loss unbearable. This can add secondary losses, leading to marriage problems, even separation or divorce.

Both men's and women's styles of grief have something to offer, although the extremes can be unhealthy. It is helpful to get away from the hard emotional work of grieving for short periods of time, and to invest some energy back into life by coping with everyday reality. It may be that zigzagging back and forth is the best way forward for both men and women: facing the pain at times, doing some grief work, then shifting to coping, getting on with everyday life, and avoiding the raw pain.

Eventually we recover from grief by integrating the experience of loss into ourselves. The loss does not go away, but the rest of life grows larger around it, and can safely contain it. Over time, we find that we can reattach to life, to others, to God, though this can be a long, long process. People differ about when they think grief is over. Two years of working through a major bereavement is perhaps the very minimum. Some say it is never over; the raw pain can always be awakened.

Others would say that people are making a good recovery when they begin to incorporate into themselves what the lost person meant to them, and hold it as their own legacy from the relationship. We perhaps glimpse this in the detailed Genesis account of Joseph's weeping – the stages through which he came to embrace his grief. Seeing Benjamin's face seems to have been necessary to him – restoring to him the lost Face of his mother, the Face that from his birth had made sense of him.

Recent research suggests that healthy grieving is grieving which finds a way to go on relating to those who have died, not cutting them out of our minds and hearts as if they'd never existed. We do no one any good by politely avoiding the topic of death, calling it something else, or avoiding the topic. What is helpful to grieving people is talking about the person who has died – talking, talking, talking – letting many people fill out our picture of the deceased in a realistic way, helping us to incorporate a truthful picture of who that person really was to us and to others, in all their complexity.

In grief, we have to go through the door, from how life once was, through a disorienting, wrenching transition phase, to a new life. Arnold van Gennep, a French social anthropologist working in the early years of the twentieth century, studied the way people in tribal cultures negotiated important changes in their lives. He noticed that a door or gate became a symbol for changes which had to be negotiated by different members of one tribe, for both small, everyday events and for larger, more significant occasions within a village. A man inside his homestead might be both a father and husband, while outside the village he might need to become a hunter and warrior. Somehow, he had to make the change from being seen by others inside the village as a compassionate father, husband, son, friend and storyteller, to being a detached killer prepared to use violence. Confusing the two roles would be disastrous, both inside and outside the village. So making the change explicit became literally a matter of life and death. In this village setting, Van Gennep noticed that the gate acted as an important sign of this ritual change. The way the man knew that he had made the proper change between domestic father and hunter was by passing through a physical barrier that took him from one 'world' to another. And all those around him knew the change had been made as well.

When the event was of greater significance than just the daily comings and goings of village life – as, for example, when boys made the transition to manhood, or when a new leader was being installed – the ritual needed was far more elaborate and longer. Often those making the transition were sent out of the village to return with their new identity.

The same idea, albeit differently expressed, is present in our own culture, in our customs of greeting and leave-taking, or in rituals of weddings, baptisms, bar mitzvahs, retirements, funerals. These mark change; a person is moving from one state, through a disorienting transitional state, to a new state. Both individuals and their communities honour the reality of the change, making it possible for life to go on, in a new, changed way.

Ancient cultures like Egypt marked these life changes with elaborate ceremony, helping people to traverse the painful journey surrounded by an affirming community. Out of gratitude to Joseph, the Egyptians embrace his brothers and father. Their embrace helps Joseph to go through the gateway of momentous change.

When the report is heard in Pharaoh's house that Joseph's brothers have returned, Pharaoh and his servants are pleased.

> Say to your brothers: Load your animals and go back to Canaan. Take your households and come back to me ... take wagons from Egypt for your little ones and for your wives, and bring your father and come, so that I may give you the best of the land of Egypt.

Pharaoh gives them garments and provisions for the journey back to their father in Canaan. But to Benjamin he gives three hundred pieces of silver and five sets of clothing. The brothers take note, but say nothing, fixing their stares straight ahead. Joseph sends them on their way, and says to them gently: Do not quarrel along the way.

6

Out of Egypt

Transformation

———◆•◆———

It is night. The full moon is a perfect bowl of milk; Horus' left eye is made whole once again. His right eye – the sun – shone piercingly all day, and now the care of Egypt belongs to the god's moon eye. Its creamy light spills across the dark sky, dimming the stars in its liquid.

Hathor's milk, thinks Joseph – the cow-headed goddess so loved by women. These milk-drenched stars are not like the sharp desert stars of his youth. In the dry hill country of Canaan, the stars shouted so loud that young Joseph would stumble into his tent overcome by their glory. The milk stars of Egypt are gentle nightwatchers over the land.

Bathed in this pale light, Joseph wanders his brothers' lime-washed mud-brick holdings. The brothers now reside in Goshen, delta land little harmed by drought. Choice pasture land, just as Pharaoh promised, for his father, his brothers, their servants, animals, and all their little ones. Seventy persons in all, from Canaan.

The thrumming of insects in the reeds lulls Joseph. The moon's soft touch is upon his back. It shows him his *swt*, his shadow, ever before him. He has learned that he is all these things: his physical body, his soul's *ba*, the energy of his *ka*, and this too – his *swt*, his tall shadow. Wait.

His right foot halts, in mid-air. There on his path lies a small glowing worm, pale green. Curled up like his own children sleeping. Its shy pulsating glow burns a hole through his *swt* – a tiny moon in shadow black. Joseph was about to stamp out its pale light. His shadow had blinded him. But now he sees it.

Yes, he is part shadow. Since Joseph's overseeing, Egypt is also shadowed. It is a changed land. No longer are the people required to pay tax. No more handing over hard-won bushels of grain. No more required meetings with temple authorities at harvest each year, weighing the grain to be paid in proportion to land the people own, recorded against their family name. Now the people do not own any land at all.

As the famine continued severe, Joseph collected all the money to be found in exchange for the grain that the people bought. When all this money was spent, the Egyptians came to him begging: Give us food! Our money is gone. Joseph answered them: Give me your livestock.

They exchanged their horses, donkeys, cattle, flocks and herds for food. When the year came to an end, they said to Joseph:

> We cannot hide from my lord, there is nothing left but our bodies and our lands. Shall we die before your eyes? Buy both us and our land in exchange for food. We with our land will become slaves to Pharaoh; just give us seed, so that we will live and not die, and that the land will not become desolate.

Joseph made slaves of them, from one end of Egypt to the other. Only the land of the priests remained their own, for the priests had a fixed inheritance from Pharaoh. He commanded the people to sow the fields and to give one-fifth of their harvest to Pharaoh. He made it a statute, and it stands to this day.

Pharaoh is pleased to now own all the land of Egypt, all its people and one-fifth of their harvests. He is especially pleased that the once land-greedy nobles can look only to him, and not to each other. Alliances without land are weak. Chaos has truly been averted.

The glow of the tiny worm saves it from Joseph's shadow. He steps aside, his thoughts troubled. The memory of stony faces – those reduced to landless slavery – weighs upon him. Joseph's instinct tells him to make a sacrifice. As his father would – build an altar to El and sacrifice a goat. Acknowledge before the Elohim that in order to live, you inevitably take away from the lives of other beings.

Joseph reminds himself that he used all his life's *ka* to save Egypt, and his brothers. All of Egypt has been astonished by his prowess as vizier, even if many are diminished by it. He has been a father to Pharaoh; he has saved the land. Still, he knows that in this, and perhaps other actions, he is in God's debt.

So many journeys, to and from Canaan, to accomplish this saving of lives. Joseph recalls how, when the brothers returned to Canaan with their sacks full, with Simeon as proof of their good fortune, they burst in upon their father Jacob saying: Joseph is still alive! He is ruler over all the lands of Egypt.

Jacob is stunned; he cannot believe them. But when they tell him all that Joseph said to them, and when he sees the wagons Joseph sent, overflowing with grain and with gifts, his spirit revives: Enough! My son Joseph is alive! I must go and see him before I die.

The entire family sets out on this sudden journey as if in a dream. Not one is left behind, nothing is left to anchor them here any more. After a day's journey, the pull of the distant hills and the familiar sound of crickets remind them of what they are leaving. Are they also leaving behind the promises of El? When they come to Beersheba, Jacob offers sacrifices to the God of his father Isaac, as he had done of old. He seeks his face, and God speaks to Jacob in visions of the night saying:

Jacob, Jacob. I am El, the God of your father; do not be afraid
to go down to Egypt, for I will make of you a great nation there.
I myself will go down with you to Egypt, and I will bring you
up again. And Joseph's own hands shall close your eyes.

The next day, they hasten on their journey. A full moon travels
its cycle as the tribe crosses over the desert to Egypt, stopping
often, because of the little ones.

One morning Joseph hears the word 'Habirus' shouted on
the streets once again. His brothers are back safely in the land
of Egypt. Heart in his mouth, he readies his chariot, and crosses
over to Goshen. And now he is here, to meet his father. A host
of children greets him at the door with shouts, but his brothers
are subdued in his presence. They know he has come this night
to see their father. Standing at the door in a dark clump, they
shuffle back to let him in.

The moment arrives – a still point – apart from the ordinary
flow of time. Joseph presents himself to Jacob. He sees that his
father is changed: shorter, stouter, curved over; his hair and
beard hanging like shreds of bleached flax, his mottled hands
grappling clumsily with his staff.

Jacob looks up and sees his son; his voice booms out and his
black eyes blaze. Then Joseph knows that his *abba*'s *ka* and *ba*
are still his. He rushes over, falls on his father's neck and weeps.

His weeping flows, an inchoate, wordless stream. Through
it Joseph conveys the message of his life as a lonely child,
his years of loss and terror, and now as hard-pressed vizier. He
weeps for a good while. Jacob's silence absorbs him, and meets
Joseph's longing to place his burdens upon shoulders greater
than his own.

To Jacob, this is the living proof – this truly is Joseph. He
drinks in Joseph's face, to his eyes a longer face, more sharply
defined. He measures its changes, and says: I can die now, having
seen for myself that you are alive.

Joseph collects himself and tells them he will go to Pharaoh on their behalf. He says to them:

> When Pharaoh calls you and asks what is your occupation, tell him that you have been keepers of livestock since your youth until now, both we and our ancestors. Do this in order that you may remain settled in Goshen, because all shepherds are abhorrent to the Egyptians.

In time, Joseph presents five of his brothers to Pharaoh. They say to him: Your servants are shepherds, but the famine is severe in Canaan. We have come to live as aliens in your land.

Wily Pharaoh studies them and replies to Joseph: Let them live in the land of Goshen, and if you know of any capable men among them, set them over my own livestock.

Then Joseph brings his father into the palace. Jacob slowly shuffles forward, determined, his staff striking the stone floor as he progresses towards the throne. Pharaoh leans forward. He fixes his sharp-beaked, falcon face close to Jacob's, and examines him fully.

Jacob has no eyes for the grandeur of the palace, but only for the man before him. He sees a chiselled, ageless face, fuelled by purpose and granite will; a man of emaciated frame, already mummified by the desert. A man like himself, who leads his people in the ways of his god.

Jacob ignores the loyal courtiers who hover over this meeting, fretting lest the Habiru gets too close to the king. These overfed servants, even those wafting palm and feather fans, hold in their sagging girths. They avoid being seen in profile, lest they offend the idealized images on every wall, as they vie to position themselves nearest to Pharaoh. Jacob sees none of this, but only Pharaoh's dry frame, his falcon face, his thin neck offset by the weight and impossible perfection of his gold and lapis lazuli collar.

He can see that Pharaoh is truly pious. Pharaoh recognizes the radiance in Jacob's weather-beaten face.

Pharaoh says to him: How many are the years of your life?

Jacob replies: The years of my earthly sojourn are one hundred and thirty; few and hard have been the years of my life. They do not compare with the years of the life of my ancestors during their long sojourn.

Pharaoh's eyes widen. Then Jacob reaches out a shaking, spotted hand and blesses Pharaoh, the living embodiment of the Lord of the Sky.

After this, the Hebrews live in Goshen, and multiply greatly. The waters can be heard trickling through runnels. The drought is ending, and the rhythm of Ma'at resumes. Jacob is to live for seventeen more years to see this, and to feel it flow.

When the time of his death draws near, he calls Joseph. He causes him to take an oath, placing Joseph's hand under his thigh: Deal truly and loyally with me, and do not bury me in the land of Egypt when I lie down with my ancestors, but carry me out of Egypt. Bury me in their burial place near Mamre. Swear to me.

Joseph swears as Jacob bows his head. The time has come. Joseph brings in his two sons, Manasseh and Ephraim. They tussle together, each one trying to hang back behind the other, eyes glassy with fear – they have never seen someone this old. Jacob, breathing fitfully, summons his strength. He sits up on his bed, refusing help. He tells Joseph:

> El Shaddai appeared to me in Luz in the land of Canaan, and he blessed me and said to me, 'I am going to make you fruitful and increase your numbers, and I will give you this land to your offspring after you for a perpetual holding.' Therefore your two sons, who were born to you in the land of Egypt before I came to you in Egypt, are now mine, just as Reuben and Simeon are. As for your offspring that are born to you after them, they shall be yours.

Joseph is shocked. His sons have been taken from him and reassigned. He can see that Jacob's eyes are dim with age, but his purpose is not. Yet Joseph bows with his face to the ground, and presents his sons to him.

Jacob asks: Whose are these?

Joseph tells him: They are my sons, whom God has given me here.

Jacob stretches out his right hand and lays it, not on the head of the firstborn, Manasseh, but on the head of young Ephraim. Crossing his hands, he lays his left hand on Manasseh, while his right hand is on young Ephraim, and pronounces the blessing:

> The God before whom my ancestors Abraham and Isaac
>   have walked,
> The God who has been my shepherd all my life to this
>   day,
> The angel that redeemed me from all harm, bless the boys;
> and in them may my name be perpetuated,
> and the name of my ancestors Abraham and Isaac;
> and let them grow into a multitude on the earth.

Joseph is displeased, and says: Not so my father! Since Manasseh is the firstborn, put your right hand on his head.

But his father refuses:

> I know, my son, I know. He also shall be a great people, he too shall be great. Nevertheless, the younger brother shall be greater than he. I am about to die, but God will be with you and will bring you again to the land of your ancestors. I now give you one portion more than to your brothers, the portion that I took from the hand of the Amorites with my sword and my bow.

Then Jacob calls all his sons:

> Assemble and hear, O sons of Jacob, listen to Israel your father. Reuben, you are my firstborn, my might and the first fruits of my vigour, excelling in rank and excelling in power. Unstable as

101

water, you shall no longer excel because you went up onto your
father's bed; then you defiled it – you went up onto my couch!

Joseph felt his *swt* overwhelm him. Had he cast such a shadow
in life that even his brother Reuben had been blinded by it?
By being his father's favourite, did Joseph drive Reuben to this
sorry, jealous sin – to shamefully take the women who were his
father's?

Jacob continues:

Simeon and Levi are brothers; weapons of violence are their
swords. May I never come into their council; may I not be joined
to their company – for in their anger they killed men, and at
their whim they hamstrung oxen. Cursed be their anger, for it
is fierce, and their wrath, for it is cruel! I will divide them in
Jacob, and scatter them in Israel.

Joseph is confused. Is his father speaking of their violence
against himself? It doesn't fit. Joseph does not know of his
brothers' plot against their neighbours, so long ago – their
treacherous violence against the tribe whose son had disgraced
their sister Dinah.

Jacob carries on and says to Judah:

Your brothers shall praise you; your hand shall be on the neck
of your enemies; your father's sons shall bow down before you.
Judah is a lion's whelp; from the prey, my son, you have gone
up. He crouches down, he stretches out like a lion, like a lioness –
who dares rouse him up? The sceptre shall not depart from
Judah, nor the ruler's staff from between his feet, until tribute
comes to him; and the obedience of the peoples is his . . .

Joseph listens in a dream while Jacob pronounces the blessings . . . the seashore for Zebulun, strength but forced labour
for Issachar, Gad chasing out the invaders, Dan judging the
tribes, rich food for Asher, the lovely grace of Naphtali, Benjamin
dividing the spoil.

The truth of the family story has been told in these blessings, and Joseph sees it for the first time. The praise for Judah. Does his father know that Judah interceded for Benjamin when Joseph tested them all to the limits – that Judah even placed his own life at risk in order to spare Benjamin, and Jacob? Jacob must know in some way.

Finally Jacob turns to Joseph and pronounces:

Joseph is a fruitful bough, a fruitful bough by a spring; his branches run over the wall. The archers fiercely attacked him; they shot at him and pressed him hard. Yet his bow remained taut, and his arms were made agile by the hands of the Mighty One of Jacob, by the name of the Shepherd, the Rock of Israel, by the God of your father, who will help you, by the Almighty who will bless you with blessings of heaven above, blessings of the deep that lies beneath, blessings of the breasts and of the womb. The blessings of your father are stronger than the blessings of the eternal mountains, the bounties of the everlast-ing hills; may they be on the head of Joseph, on the brow of him who was set apart from his brothers.

When Jacob ends his charge to his sons, he draws up his feet into the bed. Unable to look each other in the eyes, the brothers are silent – a silence broken only by Jacob's laboured breathing, at first dry and rattling, growing choked and drowned. The night witnesses a cruel struggle as Jacob journeys in reverse the lonely path that first brought him into life. He traverses each painful stage, back to his origin. With all his might, he relinquishes one by one the powers that join his body to life. His body fights back fiercely at every step, without words, without knowledge, until the raw resisting body is finally undone. There is nothing for the brothers to do but suffer and keep watch.

Towards dawn, stillness pervades the room. Jacob breathes his last. Joseph throws himself on his father's face and wails aloud. He kisses him one more time, but his father does not awaken. He has been gathered to his people.

Later Joseph commands the physicians in his service to embalm his father. They spend forty days embalming Jacob, for that is the required time.

Jacob is no more. Joseph's world is uprooted. The judgement, the weighing of all their hearts against the feather of truth, has been pronounced in this life. By Jacob, in this small room, not in the afterlife before Osiris and Amun.

Joseph had always thought that the battles of his family were about *him* – that he, *Joseph*, was the centre around which all the family passions circled – love, jealousy, hatred, grief.

But now he sees that he has not been the centre. All this time, the centre has been Jacob. First, Jacob's fierce bonding to his favourite wife, Rachel. When she died, Joseph took that place in Jacob's heart, and became his favourite. And when Joseph was no more, Benjamin became the new centre of Jacob's strong passions. Jacob has had a way of melding himself to those he loves – until they can hardly be seen apart from the intense bonding of his heart. Jacob too had his own *swt* – the passion of his heart that overshadowed the hearts of those around him. His brothers had finally come to accept this; Joseph can see this now, although the brothers were displaced by it, and there was no fairness for them. Yet they came to feel sympathy for their father in his imperious need. Judah's intercession for Benjamin arose from this very sympathy; Judah's loving-kindness covered over this fault-line that so defined the family.

Joseph feels a new thing: he feels aligned with his brothers in their loss of favour so long ago. He is not the only brother who has suffered.

Is this the bedraggled tribe that the great El has chosen as his own? It is.

Joseph's own story has been unwritten. Before his death, Jacob claimed Joseph's own two sons as his own. To bless them, yes, to give them an inheritance in Canaan, yes; but also to perpetuate Jacob's own name.

Joseph wonders if his own name will be erased from Israel's future genealogies, now that his father has taken Manasseh and Ephraim to be heads of the twelve tribes in Israel. He laughs, remembering how as a youngster he had seen himself as the central star of his favourite constellation. The kindly milk stars no doubt are laughing at him now. Though this is a time not for laughter.

The Egyptians weep for Jacob for seventy days. Strange, how the palace courtiers have become a comfort to Joseph, strengthening him in their acknowledgement of his loss. Through their rituals, they stand at the ceremonial door and nod towards him as he passes through with his disorienting grief. At last he is known by them, changed as he now is by his father's death. Part of his *ba*, his very self, has been lost, severed by his father's death. This is understood in Egypt, where the people die young.

When the days of weeping for Jacob are past, Joseph addresses the household of Pharaoh: If now I have found favour with you, please speak to Pharaoh as follows – my father made me swear an oath to bury him in Canaan. Now therefore let me go up, so that I may bury my father; then I will return.

Pharaoh answered: Go up, and bury your father, as he made you swear to do.

With him go up to the wilderness all the servants of Pharaoh, the elders of his household, and all the elders of the land of Egypt, as well as the household of Joseph, his brothers, and his father's household. Only the brothers' children, their flocks, and their herds are left in Goshen.

Together they cross the deserts and the hill country, braving the heat once more. Both chariots and charioteers go up, a very great company from Egypt, living side by side under the stars, near the evening fire, close to those whom they deem unclean. When they come to the threshing floor of Atad, which is beyond the Jordan, they hold a very great lamentation for seven days. The strange music of the Egyptians, their sistrums and their harps, weaves with the high wailing of the Hebrews. The Canaanite inhabitants observe this curious sight of peoples mixing, saying: This is a grievous mourning on the part of the Egyptians. Therefore the place is named Abel-mizraim – 'the mourning of Egypt'.

Then Jacob's twelve sons carry him to the land of Canaan; it is the first time the brothers move together with one heart – carrying their father's body, so light now, a dried brown chrysalis given shape by its bones. They bury him in the cave of the field at Machpelah, the field near Mamre, which Abraham bought as a burial site from Ephron the Hittite. It is the only piece of land the family owns.

Joseph's oath to his father is fulfilled. He returns to Egypt with his brothers and the company of Egyptians. Back in Goshen, the brothers now worry: What if Joseph still bears a grudge against us and pays us back in full for all the wrong that we did to him? They approach Joseph, saying: Your father gave this instruction before he died, 'Say to Joseph: "I beg you, forgive the crime of your brothers and the wrong they did in harming you." ' Now therefore please forgive the crime of the servants of the God of your father.

Joseph weeps when they speak with him this way. Can they not see his heart? Forgiveness has already been accomplished; it was accomplished long ago, even before he had opened his heart to it. This *hesed*, this loving-kindness, it seems to Joseph, is the very basis of life. It seeped through his cracks and eventually flooded him. It was hardly his own doing, though he now holds it firmly as his own.

In any case, it is not only his brothers who are saved by it. He too has been saved, made into one Joseph from all his parts: his below-ground self, his above-ground self, his *ba*, his *ka*, his physical self, and now his *swt*. With Benjamin's return, his mother's Face returned to him. And his *abba*'s Face has come back to him too, creating one great *shalom*. El has been at work, and has woven the Egyptians and Asenath deep into Joseph's life. His cup is full. He expands fully into his Egyptian name Zapheneth-paneah, which interpreted means 'God speaks, he lives'.

Seeing Joseph's determination, his brothers weep. They are safe. They fall down before him, and say: We are here as your slaves.

Joseph reassures them, speaking kindly: Do not be afraid! Am I in the place of God? Even though you intended to do harm to me, God intended it for good, in order to preserve a numerous people, as he is doing today. Have no fear; I myself will provide for you and your little ones.

After the harvest, Joseph senses the season of his life changing. Jacob is no more. The drought has ended. His dreams have proved true, although fulfilled in a way he could not have imagined.

This harvest season of life, affirm psychologists Erik Erikson, Carl Jung and James Loder, is a time of integrating what has gone before. It is a journey that takes place on several levels. On the level of identity, the task of this season, says Erikson, is to create a meaningful self-understanding out of the rubble and fury of life, avoiding despair at life's messy ending through achieving knowledge of self with integrity. All the truth of one's life is needed, the highs and the lows, the opportunities grasped, the opportunities missed. Denial of one's shadow, denial of grief, denial of any aspect of life creates obstacles to this self-assessment. As we imagine this season in Joseph's life, his self-knowledge does not lead to self-condemnation, but rather to integrity and to the wholeness of *shalom*.

Another level on this journey concerns relationships. Like Joseph, each one of us begins life in helpless dependency, in fusion with our carers. As he grew, the next stage involved separating from these vital relationships in order to find his own unique, independent selfhood. This painful separation happens not just in toddlerhood and adolescence, but throughout our lives, and for Joseph happened so acutely in the aloneness of pit and prison.

Life with its losses decentres the small ego-self. If we are attentive to this, as we imagine Joseph was in prison, the possibility for a new stage in relationship emerges – a further stage enabled when we touch our larger, deeper Self, and find that this Self, in Jung's terms (capitalizing the 'S' to show its distinctiveness from our small 's' ego-self), is a conduit to the greatest unity of all – God. This rootedness in our own selfhood enables us to come to the third stage in relationships. The third stage is one of differentiated relationships that enjoy both separateness and togetherness at the same time. We are no longer afraid of losing our self when we bond with another. Nor are we afraid of our essential aloneness; we do not seek to fuse with others in order to escape ourselves. We are no longer looking to others as objects to serve our personal needs. In mature, differentiated relationships, we are able to rejoice in the other as a separate being, and at the same time, enjoy being deeply together. We are able to see the other as he or she really is, not as beings with whom we are fused. This journey is not achieved without disappointment and forgiveness. These hard lessons are the necessary means by which we come to see that others are not extensions of ourselves, but are worthy ends in themselves. They were the means by which Joseph came to understand his family, perhaps for the first time.

There is a further spiritual level to this journey, a deepening of our understanding and relationship with God. God is found not only in those special times, those experiences of the Holy, but also in the pit, in the Void where the existence of our very self is threatened. Theologian and psychologist James Loder argues that these experiences of the Void echo the harrowing journey of birth, and the times we lost the loving Face that gave anchor to our childhood self. These deep experiences of the Void are re-evoked in life when our sense of self is threatened with annihilation. The terror of losing this sense of *being a self* – our life's most arduous achievement – is the great fear that underlies our fear of dying. Yes, we are wired to flee from physical death, it is indeed frightening, but the erasure of our worth, of our self, is even worse. Will this annihilation of self be for ever? All human civilizations find ways of defending against this threat of meaninglessness, of extinction – and find ways of ensuring a social memory of the self. Loder argues that we need not run from this dark reality; that in the Void – in this unspeakable underbelly of life – God is indeed present, though perhaps experienced as absence. It is far from easy. The journey towards the end of life takes us into these deep waters.

Pharaoh now buries himself in the work of preparation for his afterlife: his tomb, its secret chambers, the casting of hundreds of gilded servant figurines and objects to attend to his daily needs in eternity – all necessary work to ensure his afterlife, the preservation of his self, and thus of Egypt. It is assumed that Pharaoh's heart will be found lighter than the feather of truth, that he will be blessed, and will sail on Ra's solar barge into the heavens, for ever to watch over the land. His golden barge now is being crafted for the treasure room. The palace attends to little else. The palace looks only to the West, where the sun sets over the desert land of the dead. It leaves Joseph to attend to the East – the land of the living, where the Nile waters now flood at their appointed time.

Asenath is unwell. She has the river sickness, with night fevers, and the daytime languishing of her life force, her *ka*. Joseph worries, though she can still make him laugh. He thinks of her as he watches a lotus flower rise and sink along with the river's swell. An emerald-green dragonfly lands on its petals. The dragonfly has her grace, her quickness, the tilting of her head, her small chin and large eyes fixing him in her stare. He laughs and is flooded with joy.

A white blur, a swooping movement. The head is still there, but the body is no more. The body has been swallowed by an ibis. The tilting, wide-eyed face falls from the beak, expressionless.

Delight turns to rage. This dragonfly was Asenath. The one who prised open his heart and brought him the *ankh* – the key of life. Joseph strikes his own thighs with his fists. His floating worry for her hardens to anger and dread. The reeds rustle. He spies a fowler – about to capture the offending ibis with his fowler's net. Yes, kill it. Kill it.

Then he remembers that he is the vizier, the law-enforcer, who must himself intern whoever illegally hunts Pharaoh's river fowl. Whoever this fowler is, he is by statute a landless slave – trapped already in Egypt's net. We are all caught in the net, thinks Joseph. Its weave entraps us all in the end.

Joseph's anger – over the threatened end of Asenath – cannot be quelled. Its force masses inside him; he would overturn mountains for her. Joseph now understands the pyramids. No effort is too great to defeat the outrage of death. The inescapable net. No wonder the Egyptians – who love life and want more of it – bind themselves as a single shoal of fish to achieve the impossible, to create mountains that will last for ever, that will catapult Pharaoh to reign in eternity, their own link to the heavens. It makes sense, though there is no release from this infinite labour. Labour that starts at birth and continues for ever. Every aspect of the afterlife must be prepared for, every chant must be known, every incantation must be memorized, to get through each of the twelve gates of death, one per hour on the perilous journey to the afterlife. No wonder the walls of Pharaoh's tomb are covered with inscriptions, in case he forgets a single word. One mistake at any point will entrap the deceased for ever. Caught in the net of unpreparedness, his *ba* and *ka* are destined to wander, separated from the canopic jar of bodily organs, separate from its mummified form, never to become an eternally embodied Effective One in the resurrection.

Joseph is weary. The work of dying seems even harder than the labour of being born. The labour of living is wearying too. All this effort to preserve the pyramid of power. To preserve the reign of Pharaoh, and his hierarchy of nobles and priests, against the chaos of Seth. The struggle to control the forces that give life to Egypt: river, flood, sun, grain, soil. The labour of words to present this struggle as ordained by the gods. To write it down for all time: sacred and safe from challenge. And in Joseph's own tribe, it is the firstborn who will have power. But then the youngest seeks to usurp the firstborn's privileges. The firstborn retaliates. The endless struggle to overturn the pyramid of power between brothers. The struggle to grab for yourself if others have more. Power and control. Control and power. We are all caught in the net. Then comes death.

It is wearying, thinks Joseph. He wants to loosen his grip on his vizier's staff, to lay it down. Only a few things he knows for certain now: he has not been the centre; El has been with him, yes, throughout everything. Perhaps even Jacob has not been the centre. Perhaps the real story belongs to El.

This thought sits with him. Over time, in this new light, Joseph feels a quiet gratitude swell in his heart – that he has played his part, that he has seen so many wonders, so much of life, and the *shalom* that ultimately seeps through it. It rises in him, like the Nile in early flood. When he was young, Joseph used to think of El when he gazed at the mesmeric evening fire, and the glassy distant stars. Those images disappeared from his heart when he was in prison for so many years. There, truly the Elohim had no image, and could not be imagined.

And yet the heart plays its tricks. Yesterday Joseph's heart glimpsed the action of El afresh. In the marketplace, the naked children were whooping uproariously, running from stall to stall, shouting their chants and their dares to one another. One bold child raced up to a group of men playing *senet*, the board game of chance greatly beloved by the Egyptians. This imp messed the pieces around, and ran off laughing before the adults could slap away his mischievous hands. The adults conferred. The pieces could in no way be put back. The game was transformed.

Then Joseph knew. Just like El, overturning the pyramid, messing with our preoccupation with power, laughing while he transforms our game. This is the thread! This same story is told through the lives of Abraham, Isaac and Jacob, again and again. The younger, not the firstborn, prevails. Jacob usurps his elder brother Esau's birthright. The youngest gets the power of the firstborn, *undeservedly*. Young Joseph, not his older brothers, rises high. Ephraim, his younger son, is blessed first by Jacob, over Manasseh. The youngest – the least – shall be the first. It's all upside-down in the world guided by El.

Face it, seems to be the message. After that, you are sent out into the desert – to wrestle and be changed. Vizier Joseph, the unclean shepherd boy, has been part of this great overturning, this freedom to set others free. Asenath would laugh wonderfully.

It is a secret Joseph holds in his heart. The pyramid shall be overturned; the net shall be flown. Joseph's *ka* increases. With it, he lives to see Ephraim's children of the third generation. The children of Machir, son of Manasseh, are also borne on Joseph's knees. The perfection of each newborn is a dewdrop to Joseph, refreshing him in his long desert years. He is nearly one hundred and ten years old.

His stance is still upright through long habit – the balancing of his too-heavy headdress. Only his cloudy eyes and his clumsy hands reveal the toll of his years – hands that are now like his father's hands, wizened, with Jacob's slight tremor.

The palace is concerned that Joseph is making preparations only for his embalming. Where are your tomb's treasure rooms, with your clay statues of servants, and all the furniture needed for your daily afterlife? A person of your status can have all these gilded. Where are your wall carvings with incantations to enable the celebration of your body's rebirth?

But Joseph has given up this labour of control over his journey into death. Who is he to arrange the *senet* pieces? El alone knows the way to liberation.

Instead, he says to his brothers: I am about to die; but God will surely come to you, and will bring you up out of this land to the land that he swore to Abraham, to Isaac, and to Jacob. He makes the Israelites swear, saying: When God comes to you, you shall carry up my bones from here.

Much later it is written: Out of Egypt I have called my son.

Study Guide

---·•·•·---

Using this study guide

1 By individuals

At the end of each chapter, turn to that chapter's section of this Study Guide. Keep a journal and write down your responses to the questions as you work through the Study Guide on your own. Reread at intervals to observe your own story unfold.

See also the 'Next steps guide' (at end of Study Guide, on page 149), and 'Further reading' sections (in Chapter Notes, References and Further Reading, on page 153).

2 For groups – churches, book clubs, self-help groups

Course materials

Joseph **book.** Each person needs their own copy of *Joseph: Insights for the Spiritual Journey*, purchased online through Amazon, or from a bookstore. Participants are to read the relevant chapter in advance of each session. Buy in bulk for your group if that is convenient.

Study Guide. Everyone needs a Study Guide for each session. Group leaders can download the *Joseph* Study Guide from the SPCK website: <www.spck.org.uk>. Print or photocopy one for unexpected participants. Or, instruct participants to bring their own *Joseph* book to each session, to use the Study Guide in their book.

Bibles. Background reading from the Genesis account is listed at the start of each session's Study Guide. Ideally, these Genesis passages are read in advance of each session, along with the assigned *Joseph* chapter.

Arrange to have enough Bibles to look at suggested passages – particularly for Sessions 4, 5 and 6.

Group leader is a group facilitator

Appoint a group leader who is experienced in facilitating group discussion. The facilitator makes sure that the sessions are organized – that a suitable venue is arranged, times and dates are agreed, participants are invited and informed about the *Joseph* study group, and *Joseph* books are ordered. (See page 116 for a suggested Study Group invitation form that you can enlarge and photocopy.)

Feel free to appoint more than one facilitator to take turns facilitating the sessions. Do ensure all facilitators are experienced in leading group discussion. Facilitators can share observations with each other so that all the sessions are led in a way that is harmonious and positive.

Facilitating style

A good facilitator follows the Study Guide questions, at the same time allowing the discussion to unfold naturally and organically. The facilitator needs to exert some 'presence' and energy in order to keep the group engaged, but he or she is not the resident expert with all the right answers. Rather, the facilitator makes sure that no one person dominates the discussion, and that everyone is encouraged to speak, although no one is ever coerced or put on the spot. There are no right or wrong answers, and facilitators should affirm anyone who offers a comment.

To get a discussion moving that involves everyone, follow a sequence like this:

1 Pose a Study Guide question.
2 To the first person who offers a response, affirm and summarize it: 'Very good, John says that . . .'

3 Then ask, 'What do other people think?'
4 Next response is given. Repeat sequence.

People will quickly get a sense of the process, and they will join in, unafraid of saying the wrong thing. The aim is to probe the issues from multiple viewpoints. To close down a discussion so that you can move on to the next question, try to summarize the main viewpoints that have been offered, and perhaps someone will be able to weave those viewpoints together into some kind of overarching framework. It is fine if this does not happen; simply move on to the next question.

You are warmly invited to a Study Group **to discuss the book** ***Joseph*** **Insights for the Spiritual Journey** The group will meet over six sessions	
Venue:	Start date: Time:
About the book: The story of Joseph in the book of Genesis mirrors our own story. Every human being will face problems in life: relationship breakdown, depression, stress, unforgiveness, bereavement and suffering. How these crises are negotiated, and what resources are grasped, shape the turning points of life. They are fuel for transformation. ***Joseph – Insights for the Spiritual Journey*** is written by Sara Savage, and published by SPCK.	
Your group facilitator is:	
Contact telephone: Email:	
Refreshments:	

Figure 1. Sample invitation to *Joseph* study group to photocopy

If the discussion is going wildly off track or becoming bizarre, simply respond with a light-hearted 'That's interesting!' and bring the discussion back to the Study Guide questions. If someone is going on for way too long, or divulging too much private information in the context of the large group discussion, thank them for sharing and close it down in an affirming way. If in doubt, return to the Study Guide questions; the group will be happy to see the structure and direction for each session.

A good facilitator starts and stops the sessions on time, and allows approximately 30 minutes for each discussion section:

- About Joseph – discussion in the large group (30 minutes).
- About You – discussion in groups of three (30 minutes).
- About Jesus – discussion in the large group (30 minutes).

Social rules

In the first session the facilitator explains and gets agreement to the social boundaries – the social rules – that will help the group become a safe and enjoyable place for everyone:

1 No one gets shot down or criticized for what they say.
2 Confidentiality – anything said in the room stays in the room.
3 Avoid advice-giving. Empathy is more helpful than opinion.

The facilitator is responsible for reminding people of the boundaries of acceptance and confidentiality whenever needed.

Group size

An ideal group size is 12–15 participants. Divide your group in half if it gets too big, each half with its own facilitator. Eight is usually the minimum for vibrant discussions.

Not a counselling group

The sessions are not intended to become counselling or group therapy sessions. People should not be required or encouraged to divulge sensitive, private information. People should not feel they need to give each other advice; it is much more helpful to simply listen with support and empathy.

Dividing into small groups of three

Note that questions about our own lives are discussed in the context of small groups of approximately three participants. If your numbers don't divide evenly, one or two small groups can become a foursome. Week by week, try out new threesomes. It is hoped that the whole group will become a 'safe place', yet without requiring people to share deeply personal information.

What if a personal problem arises?

If the sessions elicit a pressing need in one of your participants, there is a 'Next steps guide' at the end the Study Guide, providing internet information to enable participants to carry out their own search for counsellors, therapists or spiritual directors in their area. Facilitators are not responsible for solving people's problems, but they can support people to pursue next steps for themselves. Further reading is provided in the Chapter Notes, References and Further Reading section to enable people to explore more deeply the issues the book raises.

Preparation and room set-up

The facilitator should read the relevant *Joseph* chapter and Study Guide section in advance of each session (and the Genesis passages if possible). The facilitator makes sure the refreshments are organized, and that the room is set up to enable whole group discussion. A circle or semi-circle of chairs seated around a table works well, with the facilitator visible to all. As well, clear enough space in the room for the chairs to be arranged later into small groups of three.

Bring a couple of extra Study Guides for unexpected newcomers, but don't allow the group to become too large (much over 18 participants). Divide it if it does.

Refreshments

If your group enjoys having a bring-and-share meal or refreshments before or after the discussion, this works beautifully. A meal adds time and effort to the sessions, so canvass your group's preference and timeframe.

Course duration

There are 6 chapters in *Joseph*. For a 6-session course, participants read the relevant *Joseph* chapter in advance of the session. You can slow it down if your group prefers to cover a particular chapter over two sessions. Each session's discussion (comprising all three sections) should last around 1.5 hours, not counting refreshments. Much longer is too tiring for most groups.

Session endings

Do end the sessions at the agreed time. This keeps the group's boundaries intact. If you haven't worked through all the questions by the end, canvass your group's preference whether or not to continue the unanswered questions at the next meeting, or simply to go on to the next chapter. Suggestions for ending the session are provided, but do close your meeting in a way appropriate to your group. Remind people of the next session's date, time and venue.

In sum, the Study Sessions aim to encourage:

- Honest, stimulating discussion
- An understanding of human life in different historical contexts
- Growth in self-awareness
- Spiritual development and exploration
- Deepening how we read Scripture, enriched with psychology, history and imagination
- Friendships within the group.

Have fun!

Study Guide for Session 1:
The birth of the social self

Read in advance: *Joseph*, Chapter 1 The Tent
Background reading: Genesis 37.1–20

Section 1. About Joseph   Whole group discussion (30 min.)

1 What is Joseph like as a baby? As a young child? How does he experience the people around him?
2 When his mother Rachel dies, Joseph loses his beloved Face (with a capital F). What does this mean for him?
3 What we've experienced in our early relationships is what we expect. What do you think Joseph expected from life and other people:
   - Before he was 6 years old?
   - After he was 6 years old (after his mother died)?
4 How does Joseph's position in the family (youngest, favourite) affect him? How does it affect his older brothers?
5 What were his brothers' reactions to Joseph's two dreams?

Section 2. About you   Divide into small groups of three (30 min.)

Facilitator, remind the group about the social rules, described above.

1 When we are born, what do you think we 'lose'?
2 The attachment between a young child and his or her carers is known to have a profound impact on the child's sense of self and future development. Who is the one person in your life to whom you were most closely attached as a young child? Can you recall times in your life when you felt

safe and secure with this person? Times when you didn't feel secure?

3 Who were the other important people in your life when you were growing up (grandmother, brother, sister, aunt, teacher, neighbour)? What was their impact upon you?

4 Do you think you were comforted and contained by your carers when as a child you expressed strong emotions like anger, fear or sadness? Or were you told to be quiet, or even punished, for expressing strong emotions?

5 What is your emotional style today? Do you bottle it all up? Not even feel it? Or do your emotions explode now and then?

6 All children have a strong will to survive and to thrive. How has your position in your family (youngest, eldest, in-between) influenced: How you relate to others? How you pursue your goals?

7 The above questions are about the influence of 'nurture' in your life. What temperament has 'nature' given you? Outgoing extrovert? Reserved introvert? How do you think nurture and nature combine in your case? Both moving in the same direction? Or do they modify each other?

8 As an adult, how do you generally expect other people to respond to you? Ignore you? Like you? Pamper you? Be irritated by you? Any links to your early experience?

Think about

An African proverb states: It takes a village to raise a child.

- Who are the people who have made you who you are today? Think of the positives as well as the limitations.
- To whom do you feel gratitude?
- Who do you wish had given you more of what you needed?

Section 3. About Jesus   Regather the whole group (30 min.)

1 Josephus, a Jewish historian of first-century Israel under the Romans, refers to Jesus of Nazareth as 'Jesus *bar* Mary'. *Bar* in Hebrew means 'son of'. In the patriarchal culture of that period, it would have been normal to refer to a male as *bar* (father's name), not *bar* (mother's name). What kind of slur on Jesus might be signified here? How might this have affected Jesus?
2 What experiences in life did Jesus have of being rejected:
   • By his family?
   • By his fellow Israelites?
   • By his disciples?
3 What role do dreams play in the Gospels? Look at:
   • Matthew 1.18–23
   • Matthew 2.13–15.
4 Whereas we know very little about Jesus' early life, it is clear that Jesus grew to become a person of enormous empathy. How would experiences of being securely attached to family *and* experiencing the pain of being rejected have helped Jesus to become a person of empathy?
5 Why does it help us that Jesus has experienced the kinds of suffering we experience? Explore: Hebrews 2.17a: 'Therefore he had to become like his brothers and sisters in every respect, so that he might be a merciful and faithful high priest.'

Suggested ending: Aaronic blessing

Facilitator says one line, and the group repeats it:

> The Lord bless you and keep you *(repeat)*
> The Lord make his face to shine upon you *(repeat)*
> The Lord lift up the light of his countenance upon you
>   *(repeat)*
> And give you peace. *(Repeat)*

Study Guide for Session 2:
Entering and exiting depression

Read in advance: *Joseph*, Chapter 2 The Pit
Background reading: Genesis 37.12–36 and Genesis 39.1—41.32

Section 1. About Joseph   Whole group discussion (30 min.)

1 Describe Joseph's emotional experience of:
   - The trauma of his brothers' lethal attack.
   - Being sold into slavery.

   What did this do to Joseph's expectations of life?
2 How did Joseph feel when he was thrown into prison by Potiphar? What thoughts about life might he have had?
3 Why do you think Joseph was able to be resilient in prison – to have the ability to keep on trying – even though he had lost so much?
4 Describe how life must have seemed to Joseph after the cupbearer, whom Joseph had helped to get released from prison, forgot about Joseph and left him to rot in prison.
5 Chapter 2 talks about Joseph's normal perceptions of life – with himself as the centre of things – beginning to wear away after years in prison. Does this ring true to you? Would this affect how Joseph thinks about God (El)?

Section 2. About you   Divide into small groups (30 min.)

Facilitator, arrange people into new groups of three, different from the previous session.

1 Most people feel down or depressed at some time in their life. Big life events like bereavement or loss of a job can trigger depression – especially if they remind us of past

problems. Or, a small, final straw that adds to a growing heap of mundane problems can also spark depression. What is your experience?

2 How would you describe the experience of feeling depressed? What are the physical symptoms? What emotions (or lack thereof) do you experience?

3 Cognitive biases are ways of thinking similar to wearing very dark glasses – everything you see in life is coloured with gloom; the negative is highlighted. During times of being very 'down', do you recognize in yourself any of these common cognitive biases:

- The self. I am bad, worthless, unlovable.
- The world. Other people are selfish, angry and mean, and are out to get me.
- The future. Things won't change; if they do, they will get worse.
- Black-and-white thinking. Either I get 100 per cent in the exam or I'm a failure. No shades of grey.
- Overgeneralize. If it goes wrong once, it will go wrong every time. That one error in my performance tonight means I will never, ever succeed.
- Focus on the one negative or worrying detail. The parking ticket I got this morning will ruin the trip to the beach, and the whole vacation.
- Positive experiences do not count; successes are a 'fluke'. I may have lucked out this time, next time I won't.
- Jump to conclusions. Expect the worst. When he walked through the door, he didn't smile at me; the relationship is probably over.
- Catastrophes will happen. The one error in my report means I'll lose the account; in fact I'll probably lose my job.

- Take feelings as facts. I feel so incredibly anxious, so there must really be danger. I can trust no one; my feelings say so.
- 'Should' statements. Unrealistic standards of perfection must be attained in word and deed. I shouldn't feel upset or angry. I shouldn't feel depressed. My life should be perfect.
- Personalize everything. I am at fault for everything that goes wrong. I should have solved my friend's personal problem for her long ago.

4 How does our culture's expectations of having the 'perfect life' contribute to our dread of being depressed?

5 To cope with very difficult times in your life, what means of coping do you draw upon?
- Getting support from close relationships
- Prayer
- Spiritual help from church members and clergy
- Talking with an experienced and wise counsellor
- Problem-solving, fact-finding, taking action
- Distracting yourself from the problems with sports, work or hobbies, so you can get on with everyday life
- Other?

6 In your experience, how is God at work (or not) in the dark times of life?

7 If you have gone through a difficult time in your life, has your perception of God been affected by this?

8 Do you feel that your faith matured, or do you feel aspects of your faith were undermined? Or a mixture of both?

Think about

God remains, but he is not as I thought. (St John of the Cross)

Note

If you feel 'stuck' in some aspect of your life and would like to explore those issues in a safe context, see the 'Next steps guide', on page 149.

Section 3. About Jesus   Regather the whole group (30 min.)

1 In Isaiah 53.2–3 we read about a suffering servant:

> He had no form or majesty that we should look at him,
> nothing in his appearance that we should desire him.
> He was despised and rejected by others; a man of suffering, and acquainted with infirmity (grief, in the RSV translation).

What do you think were some of the 'low' times for Jesus in his life? What do you think his feelings were? What kinds of coping strategies does he exhibit?

2 Do you think Jesus managed to stay clear of cognitive biases? How did he perceive:
   • Himself?
   • Others?
   • The world?
   • God?

3 In a relationship of faith with Christ, how can his resilience be made available to you? Think about this realistically. We often want to give the 'right answer'. How really does this happen?

Think about Isaiah 53.11: 'Out of his anguish he shall see light.'

4 Why do you think it is therapeutic for us for our Redeemer to suffer in body, mind, emotions and spirit, in the same way that we do?

Suggested ending for Session 2

Sing (or read together) one or two verses from the song, 'Brother, let me be your servant' (in *Songs of Fellowship*).

Please see the 'Next steps guide', on page 149, if you wish to explore these issues further.

Study Guide for Session 3: Stress and coping

Read in advance: *Joseph*, Chapter 3 Into Egypt
Background reading: Genesis 41.33–52

Section 1. About Joseph   Whole group discussion (30 min.)

Facilitator reads out:

> The psychologist Carl Jung describes how all people tend to wear a mask, a 'persona', presenting to the world the face we feel is acceptable to those around us. We tend to hide our socially unpreferred 'shadow' side from others and ourselves. There is some similarity here with the idea of having a 'should self' – the self we think we should be in contrast to our 'actual self' (the self we think we actually are). Christians especially suffer from this! The bigger the gap between our 'should self' and our 'actual self', the more we are likely to suffer from anxiety.

1 Joseph felt he had to hide his 'below-ground' self, and keep it separate from his 'above-ground' self. Discuss what you think this meant for him.

2 Like many people today, Joseph was a 'dual culture' person. Describe the two cultures he inhabited: Egyptian and Hebrew. (Additional note: The sacred stories, and images of the gods of Egypt are a way of describing the awesome processes in the natural world. The stories were an attempt to understand and control the natural processes upon which life depends. The stories of the Hebrews showed God [El] as ethical and transcendent, without image, yet in personal interaction with Abraham, Isaac and Jacob.)

3 In your view, why did the Egyptians think that a person who shepherds animals is unclean? The writers of Genesis mention this numerous times.

(Additional note: In ancient cultures, blood, birth and death were often considered taboo – they represented the liminal space between life and death – that mysterious, awesome space that only God can safely touch.)

4 Discuss what it was like for Joseph to live in a foreign culture, wondering 'whose stories are right' and 'to whom he belongs – his father's tribe or the Egyptians'.

5 How did people in ancient times feel towards those who had a different belief system? How do we feel about them today?

Section 2. About you   (30 min.)

Before dividing into small groups, *there is a brief discussion and activity for the whole group.*

1 Large group discussion and activity
   Facilitator says to the whole group:

   Close your eyes and imagine feeling very stressed. Perhaps some-one has threatened you, and your thinking and perception narrow down into 'tunnel vision'. Perhaps someone blames you for something – in front of others. Or someone you don't like offends you. How do you react deep inside?

   Discuss. What happens to your thinking and perception?
   The facilitator now invites everyone to stand up and move their chairs to clear an open space in the room, and reads out:

   To practise having 'tunnel vision', place your hands on either side of your eyes, like blinkers on a horse, as closely as possible – so that your vision is constricted and tunnel-like. Now, walk around the room randomly, experiencing your 'tunnel vision'. Keep your 'blinkers' on the whole time. Walk around and experience this for a couple of minutes.

   Discuss
   What did you experience?

How did you view the people you 'bumped into'?

(Additional note: This experience of 'tunnel vision' is similar to having a low level of integrative complexity [low IC] – in other words, seeing the world in very simplified, black-and-white terms. Studies show that when people feel threatened, their thinking constricts, and they see the world in a less complex way. We tend to see the threatening other as 'all bad'. Fear produces constricted thinking – the deeper part of our brain [the limbic system and brain stem] is 'shouting loud' for our survival, and the complexity of our thinking declines. We respond as vigorously to a social threat to our sense of self as we would to a charging sabre-toothed tiger! Fight, flight or freeze.)

Now divide into small groups of three and discuss:

2 Signs that we are under significant stress often show up in our body: migraines, stomach problems, backache, frequent colds, asthma, fatigue, the 'jitters', racing heart, sleeplessness . . . Discuss what physical stress symptoms you sometimes suffer from.

(Additional note: Everyone is different, and our physical symptoms often show up in areas of inherited bodily weakness – such as asthma or stomach problems. This is an illustration of the mind–body link, a two-way flow of influence between our mind and our body.)

3 Some of us bottle up our reactions to stress, others of us explode, some of us seek support from others. What is your emotional style in response to stress? A combination of the above? Does your emotional style help or sometimes hinder?

4 What typically causes you stress?

5 What ways of coping with stress do you find helpful?

6 While faith is often a great support, what aspects of religion might be unhelpful to our coping? Any links here with our 'should self'?

7 In New Testament times there was an understanding of humans having a 'higher nature' and a 'lower nature'. Discuss this statement of St Paul in Romans 7.18: 'I can will what is right, but I cannot do it.' Genesis 4.7b speaks about sin in the metaphor of a wild animal: 'If you do not do well, sin is lurking at the door; its desire is for you, but you must master it.' Do you think that our reaction to stress with lowered IC contributes to our 'lower nature' behaviour?

Section 3. About Jesus   Regather the whole group (30 min.)

1 Jesus also inhabited dual cultures. The nation of Israel was occupied and oppressed by the Roman Empire. Describe some of the tensions between the two cultures.

2 Christians understand that Jesus fully inhabits two natures: human and divine. In your experience, which of Christ's natures does the Church tend to emphasize most? Human or divine? (Or a bit of both?) What do you think the impact of this emphasis is on Christians today?

(Additional note: See Figure 2, on integrative complexity levels. It took centuries for the Church to deal with the paradoxical understanding of Jesus as fully human and fully divine, and to weave that together into a high-level integration of one person with dual natures, not as two separate persons. It is not easy for our minds to hold together apparent opposites, yet somehow this is what the personality and life of Jesus asks us to do. Our understanding of the Trinity is also a high-level integration: the one God experienced as Father, Son and Holy Spirit. [See Figure 2, IC level 5.] Low IC is normal for many people. It is easy for us humans to have a low-IC vision of Jesus, emphasizing only his divinity, or perhaps only his humanity.)

IC level 0
I see the world and my faith as I always have been taught to see it. I don't question it – it works for me, and I feel safe.

IC level 1
My previous view no longer works. Some crisis – large or small – has highlighted evil or injustice. And now I see the world in black-and-white categories – good versus bad. Perhaps I am a new convert, and now my life is a story of 'before and after'.

While this can be a moral advance, IC level 1 underpins conflict between groups.

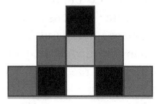

IC level 3
My previous world view doesn't work any more. Life is more complex than I thought. Now I see many shades of grey, as well as black and white. I can see some value in viewpoints different from mine. I see more of the world, and more of my faith, but it feels confusing and uncertain, and I am tempted to go back for a time. But if I go forwards . . .

IC level 5
I have found a way of weaving together the disparate parts that makes good sense. I integrate them according to my own deep values. My view of the world and of my faith is now complex, and I can understand many points of view within an overarching framework, but without letting go of my deep values. I can find win–win solutions.

This works well, but there may be times when a crisis requires me to go back to IC level 1 in order to take a stand for a time.

Figure 2. Integrative complexity levels
Note: Level 2 shows movement part way towards Level 3; Level 4 shows movement part way towards Level 5

3 Jesus did not treat people according to the black-and-white categories prescribed by the social norms of his day. Give some examples of Jesus breaking the 'social rules'. How did people respond to this?

(Additional note: See Figure 2, on integrative complexity levels. It seems quite natural to human beings to live in a 'split' world made up of black-and-white social categories, our in-group versus the less desirable out-group. For example, in traditional cultures, the sphere of men is often split off from the sphere of women.)

4 In ancient Israel, women were considered to be of a lower status socially and religiously, and were considered to be less trustworthy – a woman's testimony in law was not accepted. Do you think that ancient Egypt was an exception to this usual state of affairs in traditional culture? How did Jesus treat women?

5 See Figure 2, on integrative complexity levels. Discuss how the way we see the world, and how we see our faith, can change over time.

Suggested ending for Session 3

Facilitator says:

> You are now invited to imagine yourselves in the following story from Luke 6, in the role of the person with the shrivelled hand. In ancient cultures a physical disability was considered a source of shame and a judgement from God, for sin (either your own or your parents'). Close your eyes and imagine the scene in the synagogue, the sights, the sounds, the smells, the people gathered, with all eyes focused upon you . . .

Facilitator reads out the following Luke passage slowly, pausing here and there for 5 or so seconds after each line, to allow people time to imagine themselves in the story.

Luke 6.6–11:

On another sabbath [Jesus] entered the synagogue and taught, and there was a man there whose right hand was withered.

The scribes and Pharisees watched him to see whether he would cure on the sabbath, so that they might find an accusation against him.

Even though he knew what they were thinking, he said to the man who had the withered hand, 'Come and stand here.'

He got up and stood there.

Then Jesus said to them, 'I ask you, is it lawful to do good or to do harm on the sabbath: to save life or to destroy it?'

After looking around at all of them, he said to him, 'Stretch out your hand.'

He did so, and his hand was restored.

But they were filled with fury and discussed with one another what they might do to Jesus.

Follow this with a short time of quiet.

Close with a short prayer, such as the grace:

The grace of the Lord Jesus Christ, the love of God, and the fellowship of the Holy Spirit be with us all, evermore. Amen.

Please see the 'Next steps guide', on page 149, if you wish to explore these issues further.

Study Guide for Session 4:
Forgiveness and unforgiveness

Read in advance: *Joseph*, Chapter 4 River in Drought
Background reading: Genesis 41.56—43.14

Bibles are needed for Section 3. Also, for this session, the facilitator needs to bring: small (e.g. A5) sheets of paper, one for each participant: a large A4-size envelope, and pens or pencils. As well, bring a fire-proof metal bowl or pot, and some matches (and lighter fluid). If your venue is not safe for you to do this activity in Section 3, an alternative activity is provided.

Section 1. About Joseph   Whole group discussion (30 min.)

1 When Joseph sees his 10 brothers, refugees from famine in Egypt, he experiences a series of emotions. What do you think he is experiencing?

2 When Joseph imprisons Simeon as a hostage while the other brothers return home, a moral tension is set up in Joseph – between his need for justice on the one hand, and his desire for relationship on the other. Describe how the two cultures that Joseph inhabits (Egyptian and Hebrew) influence him here.

3 At points, Joseph seems to desire to forgive, and at other points he seems to be giving the brothers a taste of their own medicine. He seems to zig and zag between moving towards forgiveness and unforgiveness episodically. What are his motives for the various actions he takes?

4 The Joseph story takes place 400 years before the exodus out of Egypt, before the law was given at Mount Sinai, and long before the command 'love your neighbour as yourself' became normalized in the nation of Israel. The oral tradition behind this story takes place 1,500 years before Christ. Joseph is a brave pioneer of forgiveness. It's not easy.

- At the end of Chapter 4, do you feel that Joseph is to be blamed for his state of unforgiveness? What is motivating him?
- What role does 'power' play in this?
- How does having power relate to feeling safe?

5 Does Joseph have a choice in how he responds to his brothers?

Section 2. About you   Divide into groups of three (30 min.)

1 Forgiveness is a journey that each individual takes in their own way.

Work through the list below.

- Which parts of the journey do you find hardest?
- Which parts of the journey do you find easier?

(Don't feel that each person needs to experience all the points in real life, nor in this order.)

The forgiveness journey

The offence needs to be acknowledged

'You have wronged me – harm has been done by your action.' This contrasts with a state of denial: 'This didn't happen; keep a stiff upper lip, it doesn't matter, I don't matter.'

Your reality needs to be affirmed by another

If the offender is not in a place to admit to the offence, you may need affirmation by a third party who agrees that the wrong has occurred.

The offended needs to face the damage done to them

Perhaps you are permanently changed by the offence, or perhaps the world now seems an unfair place, and your faith is rocked.

The offended person has the right to feel . . .

. . . anger, rage, pain, fear, disappointment, sadness, despair . . .

The offended needs to put in place impediments against further hurt

'No, I won't allow that any more.' In some cases it might mean removing yourself from a harmful relationship. Forgiving does not mean being a martyr. To be able to forgive, you need to put the offence into the past.

The offended acknowledges that wanting retribution is normal

'This is an issue of justice: I, the wronged party, have a case. Punishment would be justified, recompense appropriate.'

Even so, the offended explores the possibility of forgiving

Perhaps you realize that recompense can never make amends or put right the wrong. Or perhaps you recognize that sin will only be compounded by vengeance. Your life is stuck in bitterness and rumination, and you want to try something new. You become willing to forgive.

The offended makes a decision to forgive

You freely make a decision to forgive – to not exact punishment or recompense. You decide that the relationship, the person, the offender is more important than getting your 'rights'. You let go of your right to exact a penalty. You opt for love rather than alienation. Perhaps you give to God the responsibility for justice in this case. You let the offender go free.

You commit to this decision

You return to this commitment whenever you are tempted to go back.

You work at forgiveness

In *reframing* the offender, you try to understand what life circumstances contributed to the offender's behaviour, how perhaps they are blind about their hurtfulness. Or, you put yourself in the offender's shoes. You *feel empathy* with them in their sin, alienation, blindness and guilt. Or, you imagine what life could be like if you could forgive, and you set out to *practise the role of forgiver*.

You deepen your forgiveness

You find meaning in not being alone in your woundedness. You become able to help others who suffer. You take action to prevent further abuse for others. You realize that you need forgiveness in life too. You find that negative feelings decrease; as you set the other free you discover that you are set free too. You don't need to avoid the offender any more. You don't have unrealistic expectations of them to meet your need, and you may even feel some positive feelings towards them. You begin to feel free.

2 About reconciliation: forgiveness doesn't require an apology, though a sincere apology is very helpful. If no apology is forthcoming, forgiveness is a free decision made by the offended. And that is a good outcome. But we hope for relationships to be fully restored, on both sides. What do you think needs to happen – on both sides – for reconciliation to occur? Think about the realism of St Paul's exhortation, as well as its high ideal: 'As far as it is possible with you, live at peace with all.'

Section 3. About Jesus   Regather the whole group (30 min.)

Make Bibles available for this discussion.

1 When the disciples asked Jesus to teach them to pray, the Lord's Prayer shows us that receiving forgiveness and forgiving others are central.

What does it mean: 'Forgive us our sins as we forgive those who sin against us'?

Discuss these possible transliterations:

- Forgive us because we are working on forgiving others.
- Forgive us unconditionally – and, by the way, we are working on forgiving others.
- Forgive us so that we are enabled to forgive others.
- Forgive us only to the same degree that we forgive others.

How do you understand this phrase in the Lord's Prayer?

2 Jesus was not a doormat. Where in the Gospels do we see Jesus directly confronting wrong? Give some examples from the Gospels (for example, confronting his disciples or the Pharisees about . . .)

3 Where do we see Jesus taking action to avoid being harmed by others?

4 Are Jesus' behaviours of confronting wrong and avoiding harm different from the act of forgiveness? Or, are they part of a longer, interpersonal, educational process instigated by Jesus that ultimately ends in forgiveness?

5 Research shows that people usually need to be able to put the offence into the past, so that they are safe enough to offer the gift of forgiveness. When Jesus was on the cross, undergoing crucifixion, the offence was ongoing, fiercely in the present. How was he able to forgive?

6 Discuss: 'Father, forgive them for they do not know what they are doing.'

Who are 'they'? What don't they know they are doing? What is it that they do not have the 'light of consciousness' about?

7 Jesus asks God to forgive his enemies here. At other times, Jesus himself forgives sin, for example with the paralysed man lowered through the roof for Jesus to heal him. In the Gospels, we see Jesus pronouncing forgiveness, and this is accompanied by healing and social restoration at the same time. Find some

examples in the Gospels of Jesus pronouncing forgiveness, and discuss the effects on the person's social context.

8 Discuss your understanding of Jesus' forgiveness. What is happening when Jesus forgives? Is it simply that he lets go of resentment and retribution? Or is it a much bigger healing?

Suggested ending activity

The facilitator passes out small pieces of paper, and provides extra pens or pencils. Have ready a fire-proof metal bowl, large envelope and matches. The facilitator reads out:

The synagogue leader who asked Jesus for more faith, said: 'I believe; help my unbelief.' We can pray along those lines: 'I forgive, help my unforgiveness.'

Who is the one person or group of persons that you struggle to forgive? Do you feel you are ready to ask God to help you forgive?

No one will see what you write; please write down that name on the small bit of paper, and fold it up.

On the Day of Atonement, the day when the nation of Israel is forgiven of their sins, the people were to present an offering to the Lord by fire.

Pass around the large envelope for each person to place their folded-up paper inside it. If the safety conditions permit, the facilitator can burn up the envelope in a metal bowl, with the participants gathered around. Use some lighter fluid if needed. Best to do this outside!

If conditions do not permit this, dedicate this envelope to be destroyed by the facilitator at home, saying words or a prayer to that effect.

To end, the group can pass the peace to one another.

Please see the 'Next steps guide' on page 149, if you wish to explore these issues further.

Study Guide for Session 5: Loss and grieving

Read in advance: *Joseph*, Chapter 5 River in Flood
Background reading: Genesis 43.14—45.24

Facilitator, please arrange for a CD-player to be in the room. Choose a piece of background instrumental music (without words or lyrics). Choose music that is slow and peaceful (approximately 5 minutes long) to enable people to meditate on Scripture. We used 'Alina' (band 1), by Arvo Pärt. The group will also need Bibles.

Section 1. About Joseph   Whole group discussion (30 min.)

1 Describe how Joseph's need to maintain 'the pyramid of power' as vizier affected his journey towards forgiveness.
2 What do you think opened the door for Joseph to get back on the road towards forgiveness? Why did he suddenly want to give a banquet for his brothers?
3 What was happening to Joseph when he saw Benjamin's face?
4 Describe how you think forgiveness and grief intertwine in Joseph's experience. Who is he grieving for?
5 Which stages of grieving do you identify in Joseph in any of the chapters?

Stages of grieving

Denial

No, this can't be happening. It isn't happening. Nothing has changed.

Yearning/searching

Where are you? I hear your voice talking to me from Sheol, but when I look, you aren't here.

Bargaining

If only you will let me escape this prison and live, I will release my brothers from their 'prisons'.

Anger and protest

Why *me*? What have I done? I hate them all. Let them suffer as I have suffered.

Guilt

What did I do to deserve this? My brothers despise me; I am unworthy of life.

Depression

There is no way back. I am cut off.

Acceptance

I know you've died, and you won't come back; but you are here, part of me. I see you in my brother's face, and in my own.

Section 2. About you   Divide into groups of three (30 min.)

Have CD-player ready with chosen CD band ready.

1 Doorway meditation.
   The facilitator reads out the following instructions to the whole group, now divided into their threesomes:

   All life involves change and loss. Even normal or positive changes, like a new baby, involve loss of the old life. It helps to have that change marked by a public affirmation of our new state and identity as we travel:

   - From our previous life
   - Through a disorienting, wrenching transition
   - To a new state of life.

Imagine a door – fill in the details of the doorway in your imagination – the texture of the wood or stone, the colour, the size of the doorway.

Now imagine a time in your life when you went through a great change – it may be a loss, a bereavement, a natural point of change in your life, or a new, positive life change. All change involves loss of the old, familiar state of life. Imagine yourself going through the transition at that point in your life.

As you imagine this time of change, were you completely on your own? Were others there to support you as you go through the door?

Music plays for 3–5 minutes while people imagine this time in their life. Fade out and stop music.

2 Second doorway meditation.
Facilitator says:

This second time, go through the doorway again, and this time, imagine going through the transition with loved ones standing nearby in support, affirming the change in your identity. Imagine God, Jesus, or the Holy Spirit there with you, supporting you.

Music plays for 3–5 minutes while people imagine this transition in their life. Fade out and stop music.

Discuss in threesomes:

3 Which of the stages of grieving (in Section 1 above) are:
 • Easier for you?
 • Harder for you?
4 Zigzagging – leaning into the expressed grieving, and then leaning away from it for a time to get on with everyday life – is a healthy way to grieve. Which is easier for you? Expressing/doing the grief work? Or avoiding the grief and getting on with everyday life?

Section 3. About Jesus   Regather into large group (30 min.)

Pass around Bibles.

1 What do the Gospel narratives tell us about Jesus' human experience during his suffering and death?
  Explore these verses:
  - Matthew 26.36–40
  - Mark 15.23–33, followed by Matthew 27.46–47.

2 What does the death and resurrection of Jesus mean for:
  - Our own grieving for loved ones?
  - Our own fear of physical death?
  - Our fear of annihilation of our sense of self?

3 How was God actively intervening (if at all) during the suffering and death of Jesus? To help you think about this, discuss:
  - Does God usually act independently of humans in an all-powerful way?
  - Does God act only through human actions?
  - Does God act through human actions while also transcending them in some way?

4 Discuss how you see God being present (or absent) in times of suffering.

Suggested ending to Session 5

Read a short psalm together or antiphonally, such as Psalm 61, 62 or 63.

Study Guide for Session 6: Transformation

Read in advance: *Joseph*, Chapter 6 Out of Egypt
Background reading: Genesis 45.25—50.26

Bibles and a CD-player are needed for this session. Choose a piece of instrumental music (without words or lyrics). Choose music that is slow and peaceful (approximately 5–7 minutes long) to enable people to meditate on the journey towards God. We used 'Due Tramonti' by Ludovico Einaudi (band 4 on the CD album, Eden Roc*).*

Facilitator, please note the slightly longer times for Sections 1 and 2.

Section 1. About Joseph   Whole group discussion (35–40 min.)

1 What insights did Joseph ultimately have about his father – about his father's strengths and his weaknesses?
2 What understanding did Joseph finally achieve concerning his brothers?
3 Do the brothers ever finally come 'clean' with Joseph? Do they ever fully apologize?
4 How did Joseph come to perceive his own place in the family drama?
5 How did Joseph understand his own shadow, his *swt*? What shadow has Joseph cast in Egypt? Note, approximately 400 years later, what is the state of the Hebrew people in Egypt? Discuss the cyclical nature of sin, between generations, between groups, between nations.
6 In what ways had Joseph been transformed (or not) by the end of his life?
7 Bonus point: Does Joseph's name feature among the heads of the 12 tribes of Israel in later books of the Bible?

8 What do you think was the Egyptian understanding of death?
9 At the end of his life, what was the nature of Joseph's faith and beliefs about death?
10 What various meanings can be given to this passage in both Old Testament, Hosea 11.1, and New Testament, Matthew 2.15: 'Out of Egypt I have called my son'?

Section 2. About Jesus   Whole group discussion (30–40 min.)

Pass around Bibles. Note that we move straight into discussion about Jesus in the large group, with a more in-depth Bible study. Section on 'You' occurs at the end.

1 Discuss the human experience of these events for both Joseph and Jesus. What are the parallels? What are the contrasts?
   • Birth
   • Family relationships
   • Journey to Egypt
   • Relations with religious leaders of his time and context
   • Fulfilling a role of influence from the age of 30 onwards
   • Suffering/rejection
   • Offering of forgiveness
   • Faith in the face of death.
2 From these passages in Matthew and Acts, what do you think is a Jewish understanding of death in Israel in the first century AD:
   • Matthew 22.23–33
   • Acts 10.6–10?
3 Bonus point: Do you find any contrasts or comparisons with an Egyptian understanding of death?
4 In contrast to the Sadducees in the time of Jesus (as in Matthew 22.23–33), the influential Pharisees (drawing on many influences current at the time) did believe in bodily

146

resurrection, at the final judgement. Discuss the new meanings that the death and resurrection of Jesus brought to his disciples. To help with this discussion, read and discuss:

- John 19.19–23
- Acts 23.6–10
- 1 Corinthians 15.21–22
- 1 Peter 1.3–4
- Romans 8.18–25.

Section 3. About you   Workshop meditation experience (10–15 min.)

CD-player is set up, with selected band ready to play.

The journey towards God.

> *Facilitator invites everyone to move their chairs randomly to different parts of the room, and to sit down. Facilitator reads out:*

Each one of us is on a journey. The last chapter in *Joseph* is about the journey towards God – our own personal journey towards death, towards our ultimate meeting with God. Some of us age-wise are closer to the end of that journey than others. Some of us still have a long way to go.

Imagine the person of God, either as Father, Son, or Holy Spirit, standing in a corner of this room, waiting for you. Visualize an image of God in that place.

You are invited to stand up, and to walk very, very slowly, inch by inch, towards that ultimate destination. At any point you can stop and sit down, to think about that journey. Maybe you are not quite ready to go forward very far. That is fine. Maybe you are ready to go all the way. This is a time simply to think about our own journey towards the God who loves us.

> *Play music. Facilitator can start walking very slowly, to encourage others. After 5–7 minutes or so, fade out and stop music.*

(Alternative option: people can remain in their seats and simply meditate on the journey towards God if you feel it is a bridge too far for your group to get up from their seats.)

Suggested ending. Aaronic blessing

Facilitator invites people to stand in a large circle.
(Optional:

> *As we say the Aaronic blessing to one another, you are invited to use the ancient Egyptian, Hebrew, and Christian hand gesture of blessing. Hold up both palms of your hands and offer them towards one another, first to the people on one side, and then to people on the other side.*

Facilitator demonstrates the blessing gesture.)

The facilitator says one line, and the group repeats it:
The Lord bless you and keep you *(repeat, with optional blessing hand gesture)*
The Lord make his face to shine upon you *(repeat, with blessing hand gesture)*
The Lord lift up the light of his countenance upon you *(repeat, with blessing hand gesture)*
And give you peace. *(Repeat, with blessing hand gesture)*

Please see 'Next steps guide', on page 149, and 'Further reading' sections in Chapter Notes, References and Further Reading, on page 153.

Next steps guide

If you wish to explore any of these issues more deeply, and you would like input and support beyond the Further Reading provided in Chapter Notes, References and Further Reading, there are basically four different 'routes' that people can explore (in any combination):

1 Church-based pastoral care
2 Professional counselling through the NHS
3 Christian counselling
4 Private counselling.

These different routes to finding pastoral care or counselling are described below, along with contact details.

1 Church-based pastoral care

There may be a recognized pastoral carer, pastoral care team, or prayer ministry team at your local church. You may simply want to talk to someone on a confidential basis. Contact details should be available from your minister.

Other church-related resources

The Beta Course (2004, University of Cambridge) is designed to support the pastoral care of churches. For a copy of the course, or more information, see <www.beta-course.org>, or telephone the administrator of the Psychology and Religion Research Group on +44 (0)1223 763005.

Retreat centres

Your minister may be able to recommend some local retreat centres, for a guided or a silent retreat. See also the *UK Christian Resources Handbook* online <http://www.ukchristianhandbook.org.uk> for details of names and addresses of retreat centres nationwide.

Spiritual direction

You can contact your local Church of England Diocesan Office for information about spiritual directors in your area. Spiritual direction is ideally a form of supportive 'accompaniment' for your own spiritual journey.

The Mind and Soul website provides useful information: <www.mindandsoul.info>.

Drs Cloud and Townsend are Christian psychologists with a wealth of helpful books and courses. See <www.cloudtownsend.com>.

2 Professional counselling through the NHS

Many people in the UK get access to professional counselling through the NHS. GPs are the 'gatekeepers' to specialist NHS services, including talking treatments, and cognitive therapy. Some GPs will not mention counselling as a treatment option during consultation, so if it is something you think might be relevant to you, you may have to raise it with your GP yourself.

Some practices have counselling services as part of the surgery, or your GP may refer you to either a clinical psychologist, or a professional counsellor. In the UK, such counselling often employs cognitive behaviour therapy, which will take place over a period of some weeks (rather than months or years).

Behavioural and cognitive therapies are based on the belief that we behave according to how we have learned to behave. It then follows that we are capable of unlearning these ways and relearning better ways. Maladaptive ways of thinking can be identified and challenged so that a person learns to view life, themselves and others more realistically. Unhelpful patterns of social interaction may be isolating a person, or keeping them from positive experiences. Healthier ways of behaving and inter-acting can be learned with the help of a skilled counsellor.

Visit <www.nhs.uk> and type in, for example, cognitive behaviour therapy, and pursue the links, or talk about this with your GP.

3 Christian counselling

The following information concerning ways of finding qualified counsellors with a Christian perspective has kindly been provided by the British Association of Christians in Psychology (BACIP).

The Association of Christian Counsellors runs a referrals service. Contact them for accredited counsellors in your area by telephone on 0845 124 9569 or by email at <office@acc-uk.org> or via their website: <www.acc-uk.org>. This is the most likely way to find a counsellor quickly.

Search the counsellors section at <www.christianpages.org.uk>. Again, we can't vouch for the quality of those listed but their qualifications are given in most cases so that gives some idea.

The *UK Christian Resources Handbook* has a big list of UK Christian counselling organizations around the country. This is no longer published in book form, but may be accessed online (<www.ukchristianhandbook.org.uk>). Basic information on counselling organizations is free, but for further details you would need to email the *Handbook* at the Bible Society (<ukch@biblesociety.org.uk>).

Type 'Christian counselling London' (or whatever your required area is) into a search engine such as Google <www.google.co.uk>. Sometimes you get some useful links. There are a surprising number of local Christian counselling organizations in the UK, and this kind of search will normally show up internet and telephone counselling too, if you're looking for something like that.

Contact the main churches in the required area – they ought to know of local counselling initiatives or individuals who offer help locally.

4 Private counselling

The other option, if you can afford it, is to see a private counsellor. You can obtain details of individual counsellors from the British Association for Counselling and Psychotherapy (BACP, formerly BAC). It is important to check if the counsellor is appropriately qualified and you are entitled to ask about their training, qualifications, experience and approach. The BACP lists the qualifications of its members and only those who have had a minimum of 450 hours of practice are eligible to apply to become accredited members.

British Association for Counselling and Psychotherapy,
15 St John's Business Park, Lutterworth LE17 4HB
Tel.: 01455 883300
Email: <bacp@bacp.co.uk>
Website: <www.itsgoodtotalk.org.uk>

You can search online for individual counsellors and organizations in your area. Join online 'Seeking a Therapist' so you know the person you will see is appropriately qualified and experienced.

Next steps: Explore your options, take your own steps

Chapter Notes, References and Further Reading

————◆•◆————

Chapter 1. The Tent – the birth of the social self

Genesis 37.1–31 (NRSV) tells the story of Joseph's early life, paraphrased and retold in this chapter. The telling of the dreams follows the NRSV closely.

Genesis chapters 29 and 30 (NRSV) provide background to Joseph's birth – concerning Jacob, Leah and Rachel.

In Genesis, the name El (meaning 'the god' or head of the pantheon of gods, as in the Canaanite pantheon) is translated as 'God' in English translations of Genesis. Many scholars consider that the Genesis oral tradition predates the revelation of God's name in Exodus as Yahweh (meaning 'I am that I am', or 'I am who I am'). In this book, El is often used in order to reflect that early period. Sometimes the plural Elohim is used.

Cultural and historical background is from:

Bright, J., *A History of Israel* (3rd edn), SCM, London, 1993.

Brown, R. E., Fitzmyer, J. A. and Murphy, R. E. (eds), *The New Jerome Biblical Commentary*, Geoffrey Chapman, London, 1993.

Descriptions of the birth trauma and the Face phenomenon are from:

Boyd-Macmillan, E., *Transformation: James Loder, Mystical Spirituality, and James Hillman*, Peter Lang, AG, Oxford, 2006.

Loder, J., *The Logic of the Human Spirit: Human Development in Theological Perspective*, Jossey-Bass, San Francisco, 1998.

Loder, J., *The Transforming Moment* (2nd edn), Helmers & Howard, Colorado Springs, 1989.

On the 'morning greeting ceremony':
Erikson, E., *Toys and Reasons: Stages in the Ritualisation of Experience*, Norton, New York, 1977.

Material on early childhood attachment, impact on later relationships, emotionality and learning is from:
Ainsworth, M. D. S., Blehar, M. C., Waters, E. and Walls, S., *Patterns of Attachment: A Psychological Study of the Strange Situation*, Lawrence Erlbaum, Hillsdale, NJ, 1978.

Bowlby, J., *Attachment and Loss*, Vol. 1, Attachment, Basic Books, New York, 1961.

Callaghan, B., 'Do teddy bears make good spiritual directors? Ignatius Loyola meets David Winnicott', *The Way Special Issue: Psychology and Ignatian Spirituality*, 42(3), pp. 19–32, 1977.

Gerhardt, S., *Why Love Matters: How Affection Shapes a Baby's Brain*, Routledge, London, 2004.

Savage, S., Watts, F. and Layzell, R., *The Beta Course: A Pastoral Care Course for Churches*, Session 2, Relationships, University of Cambridge, 2004.

Further reading

For accessible books addressing issues around healthy relationships, see:
Cloud, H., *Changes that Heal: How to Understand Your Past and Ensure a Healthier Future*, Zondervan, London, 1993.

Crabb, L., *Connecting: A Radical New Vision*, Thomas Nelson, Nashville, TN, 1997.

Hendrix, H., *Getting the Love You Want*, Simon & Schuster, New York, 1993.

Levine, P., *Waking the Tiger – Healing the Trauma: The Innate Capacity to Transform Overwhelming Experience*, North Atlantic Books, Berkeley, CA, 1997.

Miller, A., *The Drama of Being a Child: The Search for the True Self*, Virago Books, London, 1987.

Rowe, D., *Beyond Fear*, Fontana, London, 1987.

Savage, S. and Boyd-Macmillan, E., *Conflict in Relationships: Understand It, Overcome It*, Lion/Hudson, Oxford.

Chapter 2. The Pit – entering and exiting depression

Genesis 37.12–36 and Genesis 39.1—41.32 (NRSV) tell the story of Joseph in the pit and his imprisonment and dreams in Egypt, paraphrased in this chapter. The telling of the dreams follows the NRSV closely.

Cultural and historical background is from:

Bright, J., *A History of Israel* (3rd edn), SCM, London, 1993.

Brown, R. E., Fitzmyer, J. A. and Murphy, R. E. (eds), *The New Jerome Biblical Commentary*, Geoffrey Chapman, London, 1993.

Von Rad, G., *Genesis*, SCM, London, 1961.

Material on depression is from:

Beck, A., *Cognitive Therapy and Emotional Disorders*, International Universities Press, New York, 1976.

Beck, A., Rush, A., Shaw, B. and Emery, G., *The Cognitive Therapy of Depression*, Guilford Press, New York, 1979.

Rosenhan, D. and Seligman, M. E. P., *Abnormal Psychology* (3rd edn), Norton, London, 1995.

Rowe, D., *Breaking the Bonds: Understanding Depression, Finding Freedom*, HarperCollins, London, 1991.

Watts, F., Nye, R. and Savage, S., *Psychology for Christian Ministry*, Routledge, London, 2001.

Watts, F., Savage, S. and Layzell, R., *The Beta Course: A Pastoral Care Course for Churches*, Session 6, Depression, University of Cambridge, 2004.

Cognitive errors adapted from:

Davey, J., *Burnout*, Gracewing, Leominster, 1995.

Resilience:

Glantz, M. D. and Johnson, J. L., *Resilience and Development*, Kluwer Academic/Plenum, London, 1999.

Trauma, spiritual trauma and post-traumatic growth:

Collicutt McGrath, J., 'Post-traumatic growth and the origins of early Christianity', *Mental Health, Religion and Culture*, 9, pp. 291–306, 2006.

Pargament, K. I., 'On the meaning of spiritual transformation', in *Spiritual Transformation and Healing: Anthropological, Theological, Neuroscientific and Clinical Perspectives*, J. D. Koss-Chioino and P. Hefner (eds), pp. 10–24, Altamira Press, Walnut, CA, 2006.

On Jung and dreams:

Hall, J. (ed.), *The Unconscious Christian: Images of God in Dreams*, Paulist Press, New York, 1993.

Young-Eisendrath, P. and Dawson, T. (eds), *The Cambridge Companion to Jung*, Cambridge University Press, Cambridge, 2008.

Further reading

For accessible books on depression, see:

Rowe, D., *Choosing not Losing: The Experience of Depression*, Harper-Collins, London, 1996.

Rowe, D., *Depression: The Way Out of Your Prison* (2nd edn), Routledge, London, 1996.

Watts, F., Nye, R. and Savage, S., *Psychology for Christian Ministry*, Routledge, London, 2001.

Chapter 3. Into Egypt – stress and coping

Genesis 41.33–52 tells the story of Joseph becoming vizier, his marriage to Asenath, and the birth of his two children, Manasseh and

Ephraim, paraphrased in this chapter. The telling of the dreams follows the NRSV closely.

Ancient Egyptian cultural and historical background is from:

Brown, R. E., Fitzmyer, J. A. and Murphy, R. E. (eds), *The New Jerome Biblical Commentary*, Geoffrey Chapman, London, 1993.

James, T. G. H., *The British Museum Concise Introduction to Ancient Egypt*, University of Michigan Press, Ann Arbor, MI, 2005.

Shaw, I., *The Oxford History of Ancient Egypt*, Oxford University Press, Oxford, 2000.

Silverman, D., *Ancient Egypt*, Duncan Baird Publishers, London, 2000.

About ancient world views:

Armstrong, K., *The Case for God: What Religion Really Means*, Vintage, London, 2010.

Girard, R., *The Scapegoat*, Johns Hopkins University Press, Baltimore, 1986.

Ricœur, P., *Fallible Man* (rev. edn), New York: Fordham University Press, 1986.

Wink, W., *Naming the Powers*, Fortress Press, Philadelphia, PA, 1984.

Stress, brain, cognitive constriction, 'black-and-white thinking':

Badcock, C., *Evolutionary Psychology: A Critical Introduction*, Polity Press, Cambridge, 2000.

Davey, J., *Burnout*, Gracewing, Leominster, 1995.

Haidt, J., 'The emotional dog and its rational tail: a social intuitist approach to moral judgement', *Psychological Review*, 108(4), pp. 814–34, 2001.

LeDoux, J. E., *The Emotional Brain: The Mysterious Underpinnings of Emotional Life*, Simon & Schuster, New York, 1996.

Loevinger, J., *Paradigms of Personality*, W. H. Freeman and Co., Basingstoke, 1987.

Rosenhan, D. and Seligman, M. E. P., *Abnormal Psychology* (3rd edn), Norton, London, 1995.

Rowe, D., *Beyond Fear*, Fontana, London, 1987.

Ryckman, R. M., *Theories of Personality* (5th edn), Brooks/Cole Publishing Co., Pacific Grove, CA, 1993. See chapter on Eysenck.

Savage, S. and Boyd-Macmillan, E., *Conflict in Relationships: Understand It, Overcome It*, Lion/Hudson, Oxford, 2010.

Savage, S., Liht, J. and Williams, R., 'Being Muslim being British: preventing extremist violence through raising Integrative Complexity', in *The Intangibles of Security*, M. Sharpe (ed.). NATO publication, IOS Press, NL, in press 2011.

Suedfeld, P., Guttieri, K. and Tetlock, P. E., 'Assessing integrative complexity at a distance: archival analyses of thinking and decision making', in *The Psychological Assessment of Political Leaders: with Profiles of Saddam Hussein and Bill Clinton*, J. M. Post (ed.), pp. 246–72, University of Michigan Press, Ann Arbor, MI, 2003.

Watts, F., Savage, S. and Layzell, R., *The Beta Course: A Pastoral Care Course for Churches*, Session 8, Stress and Coping, University of Cambridge, 2004.

Coping with stress, religious coping:

Pargament, K. I., *The Psychology of Religious Coping*, Guilford Press, London, 1997.

Pargament, K. I., 'Spiritual struggles as a fork in the road to healthy living', *Human Development*, 27, pp. 5–13, 2006.

Further reading

For accessible books on stress and coping, see:

Davey, J., *Burnout*, Gracewing, Leominster, 1995.

Plant, J. and Stephenson, J., *Beating Stress, Anxiety and Depression*, Piatkus Books, London, 2008.

Rowe, D., *Beyond Fear*, Fontana, London, 1987.

Savage, S. and Boyd-Macmillan, E., *Conflict in Relationships: Understand It, Overcome It*, Lion/Hudson, Oxford, 2010.

Chapter 4. River in Drought – forgiveness and unforgiveness

Genesis 41.56—43.14 tells the story of Joseph meeting his famine-refugee brothers in Egypt, and the events that follow, paraphrased in this chapter. The dialogue between Joseph, his brothers and Jacob follows the NRSV closely, except for changes to verb tense, and omission of some repeated detail.

Ancient Egyptian cultural and historical background is from:

James, T. G. H., *The British Museum Concise Introduction to Ancient Egypt*, University of Michigan Press, Ann Arbor, MI, 2005.

Shaw, I., *The Oxford History of Ancient Egypt*, Oxford University Press, Oxford, 2000.

Silverman, D., *Ancient Egypt*, Duncan Baird Publishers, London, 2000.

About ancient world views:

Armstrong, K., *The Case for God: What Religion Really Means*, Vintage, London, 2010.

Gellner, E., *Plough, Sword and Book: The Structure of Human History*, Collins Harvill, 1988.

Girard, R., *The Scapegoat*, Johns Hopkins University Press, Baltimore, 1986.

Ricœur, P., *Fallible Man* (rev. edn), New York: Fordham University Press, 1986.

Wink, W., *Naming the Powers*, Fortress Press, Philadelphia, PA, 1984.

On affliction:

Springsted, E. O. (ed.), *Simone Weil: Selected Writings*, Orbis Books, Maryknoll, NY, 1998.

Material on forgiveness and unforgiveness:

Enright, R. and North, J. (eds), *Exploring Forgiveness*, University of Wisconsin Press, Madison, WI, 1998.

Jones, L. G., *Embodying Forgiveness*, Grand Rapids, Michigan, 1995.

Smedes, L., *Forgive and Forget: Healing the Hurts We Don't Deserve*, Harper & Row, San Francisco, 1988.

Watts, F. and Gulliford, E. (eds), *Forgiveness in Context: Theology and Psychology in Creative Dialogue*, T. & T. Clark International, London, 2004.

Watts, F., Nye, R. and Savage, S., *Psychology for Christian Ministry*, Routledge, London, 2002.

Watts, F., Savage, S. and Layzell, R., *The Beta Course: A Pastoral Care Course for Churches*, Session 4, Forgiveness and Reconciliation, University of Cambridge, 2004.

Worthington, E. L., *Dimensions of Forgiveness: Psychological Research and Theological Speculations*, Templeton Foundation Press, Philadelphia, PA, 1998.

Worthington, E. L., *Forgiveness and Reconciliation: Theory and Application*, Brunner/Routledge, New York, 2006.

Worthington, E. L., *Forgiveness: Theory, Research and Practice*, Guilford Press, New York, 2000.

Further reading

Accessible reading on forgiveness:

Enright, R. D., *Forgiveness is a Choice: A Step by Step Process for Resolving Anger and Restoring Hope*, American Psychological Association, APA Life Tools, Washington, DC, 2001.

McCollough, M. E., Sandage, S. J. and Worthington, E., *To Forgive is Human: How to Put Your Past in the Past*, Inter-Varsity Press, Downers Grove, IL, 1997.

Smedes, L., *Forgive and Forget: Healing the Hurts We Don't Deserve*, Harper & Row, San Francisco, 1988.

Chapter 5. River in Flood – loss and grieving

Genesis 43.15—45.24 tells the story of Joseph's brothers returning to Egypt for more grain, the banquet at Joseph's house, and the first stage of their reconciliation, retold and paraphrased in this chapter. Dialogue between Joseph and his brothers follows the NRSV closely.

Ancient Egyptian cultural background is from:

James, T. G. H., *The British Museum Concise Introduction to Ancient Egypt*, University of Michigan Press, Ann Arbor, MI, 2005.

Shaw, I., *The Oxford History of Ancient Egypt*, Oxford University Press, Oxford, 2000.

About loss and grieving:

Bowlby, J., *Attachment and Loss*, Vol. 1, Attachment, Hogarth Press, London, 1969.

Bowlby, J., *Attachment and Loss*, Vol. 2, Separation, Hogarth Press, London, 1973.

Bowlby, J., *The Making and Breaking of Affectional Bonds*, Tavistock, London, 1979.

Grainger, R., *The Social Symbolism of Grief and Mourning*, Kingsley, London, 1998.

Kübler-Ross, E., *On Death and Dying*, Macmillan, New York, 1970.

Parkes, C. M., *Bereavement: Studies in Grief in Adult Life*, Penguin, London, 1986.

Raphael, B., *The Anatomy of Bereavement*, Basic Books, New York, 1984.

Stroebe, M. and Schut, H., 'The dual process model of coping with bereavement: rationale and description', *Death Studies*, 23, pp. 197–224, 1999.

Van Gennep, A., *The Rites of Passage*, University of Chicago Press, Chicago, 1960.

Walter, T., *Funerals and How to Improve Them*, London: Hodder & Stoughton, 1990.

Watts, F., Savage, S. and Layzell, R., *The Beta Course: A Pastoral Care Course for Churches*, Session 7, Loss and Change, University of Cambridge, 2004.

Further reading

Barns, M. C., *When God Interrupts: Finding New Life through Unwanted Change*, Inter-Varsity Press, Nottingham, 1996.

Kübler-Ross, E. and Kessler, D., *On Grief and Grieving: Finding Meaning in Grief through the Five Stages of Loss*, Simon & Schuster, New York, 2005.

Yancey, P., *Soul Survivor*, Doubleday, New York, 2001.

Yancey, P., *Where Is God When It Hurts?* Zondervan, London, 2001.

Chapter 6. Out of Egypt – transformation

Genesis 45.16—50.26 tells the story of Jacob's arrival in Egypt, his death and burial, and Joseph's final years, paraphrased in this chapter. Dialogue follows the NRSV very closely.

Culture as a defence against death anxiety:

Bassett, J. F., 'Does threatening valued components of cultural world-view alter explicit and implicit attitudes about death?' *Individual Differences Research*, 3(4), pp. 260–8, 2005.

Ancient culture and 'the powers':

Shaw, I., *The Oxford History of Ancient Egypt*, Oxford University Press, Oxford, 2000.

Wink, W., *Unmasking the Powers*, Fortress Press, Philadelphia, 1986.

On the last stage of life:

Erikson, E., *The Life Cycle Completed*, W. W. Norton and Co., New York, 2000.

Kübler-Ross, E., *Death, the Final Stage of Growth*, Prentice Hall, Englewood Cliffs, NJ, 1975.

Loder, J., *The Logic of the Human Spirit: Human Development in Theological Perspective*, Jossey-Bass, San Francisco, 1998.

Loder, J., *The Transforming Moment* (2nd edn), Helmers & Howard, Colorado Springs, 1989.

Young-Eisendrath, P. and Miller, M. E. (eds), *A Psychology of Mature Spirituality: Integrity, Wisdom, Transcendence*, Routledge, New York, 2000.

On psychology and spirituality:

Batson, C. D., Schoenrade, P. and Ventis, W. L., *Religion and the Individual: A Social Psychological Perspective*, Oxford University Press, New York, 1993.

Browning, D. S., *Reviving Christian Humanism: The New Conversation on Spirituality, Theology and Psychology*, Fortress Press, Minneapolis, MN, 2010.

Bryant, C., *Jung and the Christian Way*, Darton, Longman & Todd, London, 1983.

Christian, C., *In the Spirit of Truth: A Reader in the Work of Frank Lake*, Darton, Longman & Todd, London, 1991.

Frankl, V., *Man's Search for Meaning*, Hodder & Stoughton, London, 1964.

Meissner, W. W., *Psychoanalysis and Religious Experience*, Yale University Press, New Haven, 1984.

Schults, L. and Sandage, S., *Transforming Spirituality: Integrating Psychology and Theology*, Baker Academic, Grand Rapids, MI, 2006.

Watts, F., *Psychology and Theology*, Ashgate, Aldershot, 2002.

Watts, F., *The Psychology of Religious Experience*, Cambridge University Press, Cambridge, 1998.

Watts, F., Savage, S. and Layzell, R., *The Beta Course: A Pastoral Care Course for Churches*, Sessions 9 and 10, Suffering and Wholeness; Self and God, University of Cambridge, 2004.

Woodward, J. and Pattison, S. (eds), *The Blackwell Reader in Pastoral and Practical Theology*, Oxford: Blackwell, 2000. Chapters on Jung in particular.

Further reading

Bryant, C., *Jung and the Christian Way*, Darton, Longman & Todd, London, 1983.

Frankl, V., *Man's Search for Meaning*, Hodder & Stoughton, London, 1964.

Rowe, D., *Beyond Fear*, Fontana, London, 1987.

Savage, S. and Boyd-Macmillan, E., *Conflict in Relationships: Understand It, Overcome It*, Lion/Hudson, Oxford, 2010.

Watts, F. (ed.), *Jesus and Psychology*, Darton, Longman & Todd, London, 2006.